TWAYNE'S WORLD AUTHORS SERIES

A Survey of the World's Literature

Sylvia E. Bowman, Indiana University
GENERAL EDITOR

ARGENTINA

John P. Dyson, Indiana University
EDITOR

Ernesto Sábato

(TWAS 123)

TWAYNE'S WORLD AUTHORS SERIES (TWAS)

The purpose of TWAS is to survey the major writers —novelists, dramatists, historians, poets, philosophers, and critics—of the nations of the world. Among the national literatures covered are those of Australia, Canada, China, Eastern Europe, France, Germany, Greece, India, Italy, Japan, Latin America, New Zealand, Poland, Russia, Scandinavia, Spain, and the African nations, as well as Hebrew, Yiddish, and Latin Classical literatures. This survey is complemented by Twayne's United States Authors Series and English Authors Series.

The intent of each volume in these series is to present a critical-analytical study of the works of the writer; to include biographical and historical material that may be necessary for understanding, appreciation, and critical appraisal of the writer; and to present all material in clear, concise English—but not to vitiate the scholarly content of the work by doing so.

Ernesto Sábato

By HARLEY D. OBERHELMAN

Texas Tech University

Twayne Publishers, Inc. :: New York

Preface

The twentieth century has witnessed the coming of age of *belles–lettres* in Hispanic America, the advent of which was announced by the first efforts of the Modernists some fifteen years before the turn of the century. While evidence of this development may be found in every nation of the New World, it is in the centers of great literary and publishing activity—Argentina, Brazil, and Mexico—where some of the most significant figures have appeared on the literary horizon. There is no doubt that Ernesto Sábato is one of the most widely read figures of this generation, and there is indisputable evidence in the fact that his novels have been translated into some eight languages, that his works have won an audience beyond the confines of his native Argentina.

It was in 1945 that Sábato was to make his debut into the literary world with a volume of essays which won the Premio Municipal.[1] His reputation as a writer was firmly established in 1948 with the publication of his first novel, *El túnel* (The Tunnel, translated to English as *The Outsider*), a novel which has subsequently become a classic in contemporary Argentine letters and which has been translated into the major Western languages and into Japanese. It has also been made into a film which enjoyed limited success. Although Sábato continued to publish volumes of essays after the success of his first novel, it was the monumental *Sobre héroes y tumbas* (*Concerning Heroes and Tombs*, 1961) which clearly placed him in the category of the major novelists of the twentieth century. This second novel became an immediate best seller and inspired a great deal of critical comment in the international press. An Italian edition elicited such favorable comment that Sábato made a tour of Italy in 1966 in response to the demands of his newly found audience. Additional translations of *Sobre héroes y tumbas* are in preparation, and excerpts from one of its historical episodes have been made available to the public in the form of a recording which has had widespread distribution.

In spite of an English edition of *El túnel* and considerable attention to Sábato in various literary journals and newspapers, no definitive study of his essays and novels has been published in English. It is the aim of the present work to fill this lacuna and to offer one of the first book-length studies of his literary production. Throughout this analysis the point of emphasis will always be on the novels themselves and on the essays as they are related to the theses developed in the novels; no attempt will be made to study the many articles which Sábato has published in various periodicals and newspapers in Argentina and elsewhere.

While the volumes of essays and the two novels will be considered separately, an attempt will be made to draw general conclusions concerning Sábato's two principal preoccupations: a definition of contemporary Argentina together with an analysis of its problems, and a study of twentieth-century man and his relationship to a world dominated by science and reason. In the end, however, it will be demonstrated that Sábato himself is the protagonist of all his works and that, while he is both national and universal in his choice of themes, he is at all times engaging in a probing analysis of himself as the only human being of whom he can speak with complete authority.

Texas Tech University   HARLEY D. OBERHELMAN
Lubbock, Texas

Acknowledgments

The author hereby wishes to acknowledge his sincere gratitude to the many people both in Argentina and the United States who contributed in many ways to the collection and assembly of the basic bibliography which made this study possible. To John Fred Petersen appreciation is expressed for granting permission to quote from his doctoral dissertation, "Ernesto Sábato: Essayist and Novelist." Acknowledgment is also made of the permission granted to the author by Alfred A. Knopf, Inc. to quote various passages from Harriet de Onís's translation of *El túnel*, published under the title *The Outsider* as one of the Borzoi series. Finally, the author wishes to recognize the debt he owes to Sábato himself, whose many letters and critical analysis of the manuscript of this study were of invaluable assistance as was the encouragement he so kindly gave during the period of its writing.

Contents

Chronology

1911   Ernesto Sábato born in Rojas, a small town in the province of Buenos Aires some 160 miles west of the capital city.

1924–
1928   Student in the Colegio Nacional, an adjunct of the Universidad Nacional de La Plata.

1929–
1936   Student of science and mathematics at the Universidad Nacional de La Plata. During the years 1934–35 Sábato attended a Communist student congress in Brussels, later going to Paris after his disillusionment with communism.

1937   Completed the doctorate at the Instituto de Física in La Plata.

1938   Received scholarship to study radiation at the Curie laboratory in Paris. Began "La fuente muda," sections of which appeared in *Sur* in 1947.

1939   Studied and did research at the Massachusetts Institute of Technology.

1940   Returned to Argentina and published his first literary efforts in *La Nación* and *Sur*.

1940–
1945   Held professorship of theoretical physics at the Universidad Nacional de La Plata and at the Instituto del Profesorado Secundario in Buenos Aires. Resigned under pressure from the Perón dictatorship.

1945   Published the prize winning volume of essays, *Uno y el universo*.

1947   Named to an executive post with UNESCO in Paris and Rome. Resigned two months later because of dislike for bureaucratic nature of the position.

1948   *El túnel* published by *Sur*.

1951   *Hombres y engranajes* published by Emecé.

1953   *Heterodoxia* published.

1955   Named to post of editor of the popular review, *Mundo Argentino*.

1956   Publication of *El otro rostro del peronismo* and *El caso Sábato*, both studies of the unsettled political situation during and after the Perón period.

1958–   Named Director of Cultural Relations of the Ministry
1959   of Foreign Relations and Culture under the Frondizi regime. Resigned in 1959 due to dissatisfaction with governmental policy.

1961   *Sobre héroes y tumbas* published by Fabril.

1962   Sábato journeys to Europe on lecture tour.

1963   *El escritor y sus fantasmas* and *Tango, Discusión y Clave* published.

An Outline of Argentine History

1516   River Plate discovered by Juan Díaz de Solís. Almost three centuries of colonialism under Spain began.

1536   First founding of Buenos Aires. City was abandoned a few years later but re-established in 1580 by colonists from Asunción, Paraguay.

1776   Spain established the Viceroyalty of the River Plate.

1806– 1807   British troops invaded Buenos Aires in an attempt to wrest control of the city and surrounding region. Citizens of the city defeated the invaders in 1807.

1810   The Revolution of May (May 25, 1810) established independence of the Argentine provinces from the French authorities who had seized the Spanish throne in 1808. Formal independence declared by the Congress of Tucumán on July 9, 1816.

1824   Election of Unitarian president Bernardino Rivadavia who was forced to flee Argentina following year by Federalist opposition.

1826   General Juan Lavalle revolted against Manuel Dorrego, the Federalist successor to Rivadavia as governor of the province of Buenos Aires and *de facto* president of Argentina. Assassination of Dorrego by Lavalle in 1828 precipitated civil conflict of the Rosas era between Unitarians seeking to establish a strong central government and Federalists favoring a loose political alliance of the provinces.

1829– 1852   Presidency of the Federalist, Juan Manuel Rosas, who later became virtual dictator of the entire nation. Lavalle became active opponent of Rosas and began a series of campaigns through the major provinces of the north. Lavalle forced to flee northward toward the Bolivian border and was shot by Federalist patrol in the province of Jujuy on October 8, 1841. Final defeat of Rosas and the Federalists in the Battle of Monte Caseros on February 3, 1852.

1853– Representative constitution approved followed by a
1874   series of Unitarian presidencies: 1853–59, Justo José Urquiza; 1862–68, Bartolomé Mitre; 1868–74, Domingo Faustino Sarmiento.

1880   Buenos Aires officially designated federal capital.

1890   Series of conservative governments favoring wealthy landed elements began. The Radical party (Unión Cívica Radical) formed by Hipólito Yrigoyen in 1891 as an opposition party with strong middle-class orientation.

1912   Under Radical pressure the Sáenz Peña Law making vote secret, universal, and obligatory was passed, thereby making possible a Radical victory in the elections four years later.

1916– Series of Radical presidencies with significant social
1928   reform: 1916–22, first presidency of Yrigoyen; 1922–28, Marcelo T. de Alvear; 1928–30, second term of Yrigoyen now old and ineffectual. During Radical era Socialist, Anarchist, and Communist parties grew rapidly as opposition groups to the dominant political power. In 1930 a military-conservative coalition revolted to terminate the presidency of Yrigoyen.

1930– Political confusion under a series of military govern-
1945   ments. In 1943 a group of military officers under Colonel Juan Domingo Perón seized the government.

1946– Perón emerged victorious over feuding military offi-
1955   cials and was elected president. Consolidated power behind labor unions with assistance of wife, Eva Duarte de Perón, who died of cancer in 1952. Shortly thereafter discontent against Perón on the part of military and Church elements began. Labor unions reacted in 1955 by burning many churches in Buenos Aires. Perón forced to flee Argentina as his forces crumbled.

1955– Provisional military governments first under General
1958   Lonardi and later under General Pedro Aramburu.

1958–
1966
Series of governments under various factions of Radical party: 1958–62, Arturo Frondizi; 1962–63, José María Guido installed as provisional Radical president by military forces unhappy with Frondizi's liberal attitude toward Peronists; 1963–66, presidency of Arturo Illia whose term was cut short by a military coup.

1966–
1970
Provisional presidency of General Juan Carlos Onganía. Military coup in June, 1970 removed Onganía from office; Brigadier General Roberto Marcelo Levingston named by military junta to succeed Onganía.

CHAPTER 1

Sábato and His Universe

WRITING in his first collection of published essays, Ernesto Sábato states that to a certain degree every painting is a self-portrait and every literary work an autobiography. Indeed, if one were to attempt to reconstruct the biography of Argentina's most discussed contemporary novelist on the basis of facts gleaned from his collections of essays and two novels, he would find a wealth of material directly related to the task at hand. But as the thread of Sábato's life is revealed, so is the history of twentieth-century Argentina and the anguish of its some twenty million inhabitants. While the struggles, defeats, and occasional victories depicted all take place in Argentina, they are at the same time common to man in the Western world, and Sábato thereby assumes the role of spokesman for a significant segment of humanity.

Sábato's life may conveniently be considered in three divisions. His childhood in a small town some one hundred and sixty miles west of Buenos Aires and his secondary education in the provincial capital of La Plata form the first division. The details of this period will receive more than cursory attention since Sábato believes that it is most difficult to write anything profound that is not intimately linked to one's childhood. A second division will cover the years during which his life was dedicated to the pursuit of scientific knowledge. His disenchantment with the world of science occurred in 1938, after which he devoted his life to the cultivation of literature as man's most effective tool for explaining himself and his circumstance. A consideration of his literary career will form the last division of this chapter.

I The Boy from the Pampa

For one so univerasl in his discussions of mankind and its problems, it is remarkable that the first twelve years of Sábato's life should have been spent in the microcosmic world of the pampean town of Rojas, located on the west bank of a stream of the same name and on the branch line of the central railroad system. The larger cities of Pergamino and Junín are located, respectively, at the northern and southern terminal points of this system. As the county seat of a district in the province of Buenos Aires, it contained fewer than five thousand inhabitants at the time of Sábato's birth on June 24, 1911. An agricultural and stock-raising center, its population had increased by the middle of the twentieth century to 8,700, and the importance of Rojas as a railroad center was still significant.

Founded in 1779 as a fort in the struggle against the Indians of the region, its growth was slow and uneven for the next century. Even during the second decade of the twentieth century Sábato remembers it as a tranquil village where the native Creoles considered time as something to be "killed" and resisted the more energetic tendencies of the flood of Europeans who sought to industrialize Argentina and to regulate their lives with clocks. Sábato still shows a genuine disregard for punctuality which he ironically describes as a fetish invented by the Swiss.

The tenth of eleven children, Sábato was born into a bourgeois, well-established family of Italian immigrants who owned the village flour mill. Although the Sábato children were subject to strict parental discipline, they nevertheless received a solid education and an excellent preparation for life. During these first years spent in Rojas, Sábato was subjected to the rancor of his Creole peers who resisted, even cursed, the *gringos*[1] for their efforts to forge a new existence for themselves on the wind-swept pampas.

From the earliest years of childhood Sábato showed a firm inclination toward arts and letters, an inclination which led him in the essay *Hombres y engranajes* (*Men and Gears*) to a kind of self-interrogation as to the reasons for his long digression into the field of science.[2] In the same essay he sought to explain his youthful involvements with communism, an unexpected by-product of his bourgeois, scientific education. His later rejection of both science and communism as answers to the problems of man brought down the wrath of both factions upon him.

The memory of his childhood has become more intense for

Sábato with the passage of time. Sábato remembers that his first impressions of socialism were those of a Romantic, somewhat esoteric movement which he associated with politicians in tophats and four-in-hand neckties. In libraries of Rojas, Sábato recalls reading Spencer, Reclus, Zola, and Darwin, whose theory of evolution he considered as strange and subversive scientifically as socialism was politically. But Rojas was participating only marginally in the vast changes which were sweeping the country. By the turn of the century Argentina had become one of the world's greatest producers of food. Better methods in agriculture and in the pastoral industries had brought about an economic revolution accompanied by the previously mentioned influx of European immigrants. Although these factors stimulated the development of a proletariat and a middle class, the oligarchy of landowners still firmly held the reins of the central government. This hold on the nation's economy was not broken until the elections of 1916 when the Radicals, a middle-class coalition, were to wrest political control from the oligarchy and to retain it until 1930.

It was during the years of Radical rule that Ernesto Sábato was sent by his family to undertake his secondary education in the provincial capital of La Plata at the Colegio Nacional, an adjunct of the National University of La Plata. Here Sábato experienced the first crucial moment of his life, a period of anguish and uncertainty owing to his having been sent from Rojas to what for him was a huge, terrifying city. He recalls his experiences in the following words:

> I found myself alone and unprotected, far from my mother, surrounded by children who knew each other, who seemed brilliant, who could only consider a country boy with ironic superiority. I had been pathologically introverted, my nights were populated by frightening nightmares and hallucinations, and all of this interior nocturnal tumult remained within me, hidden somewhat by my timidity. On finding myself in a more difficult world, these complications were aggravated to a degree difficult to imagine, and I spent long hours hesitating and weeping. (*Escritor*, pp. 9–10)

Suddenly the field of mathematics presented a solution to the young student, a means of establishing order in a world

of chaos. The demonstration of theorems and the analysis of
geometric forms were seized upon ecstatically as an escape
from an adolescent world of desperation and uncertainty. A
key was thereby provided for entry into a world which was to
provide for a period a certain measure of tranquillity until
such time as it too was to fall asunder under the pressure
of doubt and disillusionment.

II *A Disquieting Career in Science*

With a career in science and mathematics in mind, Sábato
entered the Institute of Physics of the National University
of La Plata in 1929, the year following the termination of
his secondary education at the Colegio Nacional. In the
university he was caught up in various political and revolutionary student movements, first associating himself with
Anarchists and later with leftist groups. In 1934 and 1935 as
a delegate of the Communist youth movement of Argentina
he was sent to an international congress in Brussels where he
experienced a second crucial moment in his life, described in
some detail in *El escritor y sus fantasmas* (*The Writer and His
Ghosts*) as a series of grave doubts and uncertainties somewhat
similar to his fears upon first arriving in La Plata from the
province.[3] These fears stemmed from the fact that he was
scheduled to continue from Brussels on to the Soviet Union,
but in a moment of anguish and tumult he had fled to Paris
without seeking permission from his superiors. There, penniless
and without friends, he faced a tremendous spiritual crisis. For
a time he was befriended by the Communist *concierge* of the
École Normale Supérieure where he was permitted to sleep
until such time when he was fraternally adopted by several
Venezuelan students.

At the height of his desperation, Sábato went to the Gibert
bookstore and stole a book dealing with mathematical analysis.
In Paris, as in La Plata some ten years earlier, he was to discover inner peace again in the systematic world of mathematics. As soon as he was able, he returned to La Plata and
assiduously resumed his studies. In 1937 he completed his
doctorate and on the recommendation of Doctor Bernardo
Houssay was given a fellowship by the Argentine Association
for the Progress of Science to study radiation in the Curie

Laboratory in Paris. Here he worked with Irène Joliot-Curie, but his interest in science culminated in outright repudiation as he explored the more authentic world of the Surrealists, among them André Breton and Oscar Domínguez, who later committed suicide after entering an insane asylum. At the same time Sábato began to write. While still working in the Curie Laboratory his first novel, "La fuente muda" (*The Mute Fountain*), was begun. Although never published as an integral work, sections were to appear in 1947 in the journal *Sur*[4] after which the rest of the manuscript was destroyed except for fragments which appeared in a revised form in *Sobre héroes y tumbas*.

Although during his second visit to Paris Sábato decided that he was no longer interested in a scientific career, he nevertheless left France for the United States to continue radiation studies with Professor Manuel Sandoval Vallarta at the Massachusetts Institute of Technology. One result of this interlude was a brief scientific article in the *Physical Review* of June, 1939;[5] a second was the opportunity to see the capitalist machine in its greatest and most advanced form.

In 1940 Sábato returned to Argentina where he was named professor of theoretical physics at the National University of La Plata and at a normal school in Buenos Aires. In the same year he began to devote long periods of time to writing. His former professor of literature at La Plata, Pedro Henríquez Ureña, became interested in his work and introduced him to Victoria Ocampo, director of *Sur*, who published his first article in 1940. During this same period Sábato began to contribute to the literary section of *La Nación*, one of the leading daily newspapers of Buenos Aires. These dual activities, teaching physics and writing, were to occupy his time for the next five years when the advent of Perón caused his removal from the classroom because of his rejection of and open hostility to the dictator's restrictions on free speech and expression.

One may describe the second period of Sábato's life as experimental in nature. Espousing science and mathematics only to reject them later, he moved gradually toward literature as a means of expression, thereby confirming the tendencies observed during his childhood in Rojas. The fact that he remained in the world of science for seven years after having rejected it in 1938 can be explained by the fact that this was his only means of support while his second career was being launched. How much longer he would have remained as a professor of physics had the Perón regime not terminated his appointments is a matter of conjecture, but it is apparent that Sábato sooner or later would have left the classroom to dedicate himself to letters.

III   *A Journey through Tunnels and Tombs*

In 1943 when it was apparent that Sábato was to undergo a difficult transition in his life because of his decision to resign his posts as a professor of physics, he abandoned the city of Buenos Aires and went with his wife Matilde to Carlos Paz in the hills of the province of Córdoba, there to write. In an interview with Ricardo Bruno published in *Leoplán*, Sábato describes their life in Carlos Paz as rather primitive. A year later the couple returned to Buenos Aires, first renting and later purchasing a home in suburban Santos Lugares, still Sábato's official residence. It was in 1945 with the publication of his prize-winning volume of essays, *Uno y el universo* (*One and the Universe*), that Sábato made his official debut in the world of letters.

His claim to fame, although a modest measure based on miscellaneous contributions to *Sur* and *La Nación* and his one volume of essays, was sufficient to cause the executive committee of UNESCO to name him in 1947 to a post in Paris and Rome. This for him became a bureaucratic appointment from which he resigned after two months to dedicate himself to the writing of *El túnel*, published by *Sur* in 1948 after having been rejected by all of the leading publishing houses of Buenos Aires. Its subsequent success and translation to French at the suggestion of Albert Camus brought international recognition to Sábato as well as additional translations to English, Czech, German, Japanese, Polish, Portuguese, Roumanian, and Swedish and numerous pleas for reprinting rights from distraught editors who earlier had rejected the manuscript.

Until 1955 Sábato lived on the income realized from the sales of his first collection of essays, *El túnel*, and two additional collections of essays, *Hombres y engranajes* and *Heterodoxia*

(*Heterodoxy*). During the same period he gave lectures—insofar as he was able under the Perón government—and acted as consultant for several publishing houses. The fact that Sábato's open rejection of Perón's totalitarian methods of government was a well-known fact made him suspect during the last years of the dictatorship and greatly reduced his opportunities to speak out freely. But in 1955 a significant appointment was bestowed on Sábato when he was named editor of the popular journal, *Mundo Argentino*, which he reorganized and revitalized during the tenure of his editorship.

The difficult years at the end of the Perón dictatorship and during the 1955–58 interim of military rule under General Pedro Aramburu are reflected in the two short volumes of essays which Sábato published in 1956. *El caso Sábato* (Sábato's Case) was a short pamphlet published privately in which the author explains the reasons for his resigning the editorship of *Mundo Argentino*. At the same time he champions freedom of the press, something long absent from Argentina as witnessed by Perón's confiscation of the internationally famous newspaper, *La Prensa*, and General Aramburu's silencing of the opposition press during the early days of his government following the revolution. Having suffered ten years of misery for personally and openly rejecting totalitarian and demagogic persecution of half the Argentine population, Sábato's disillusion with the ensuing Aramburu government was equally intense as he witnessed the persecution and imprisonment of the *Peronistas* by the troops of the so-called liberating revolution. From his vantage point as director of *Mundo Argentino* he was forced to denounce this eye-for-an-eye justice, thereby bringing about his forced resignation.

El caso Sábato, because of its private publication and anti-Aramburu theme, had a limited circulation. A second volume of essays in the same year, *El otro rostro del peronismo* (*The Other Face of Peronism*), received greater attention from the reading public. Also, the theme was safer since it did not openly criticize the shortcomings of the revolutionary government. The work is an attempt to describe historical, social, and political trends in Argentina, and at the same time it presents a cogent plea for a solution to the grave problems confronting the nation. A historic disregard for the legitimate rights of the masses is presented as a causative factor in the rise of Perón, and Sábato offers as a solution the consolidation of Argentina into a unified nation in which the rights and desires of its heterogeneous masses are recognized.

The political vacuum created by the fall of Perón continued until Aramburu called a constituent assembly in August, 1957 to prepare a plan for presidential, congressional, and provincial elections. The most active opposition during the Perón years was the old Radical party which now divided into liberal and conservative factions. Ricardo Balbín, a candidate for the presidency in 1951, led the more conservative segment of the party, but victory belonged to the liberals under Arturo Frondizi. It was Frondizi's promises of high tariffs to industrialists, his opposition to Perón's legalizing of divorce, and a promise of amnesty to imprisoned *Peronistas* that successfully carried his campaign.

It should be pointed out that Frondizi promised many of the compromise proposals of Sábato's *El otro rostro del peronismo* even though he later was forced to call out the armed forces to break up strikes called by the fallen dictator from his exile in the Dominican Republic. Sábato was closely involved with the Frondizi administration in which he held an appointive post; in 1958 he had been named Director of Cultural Relations in the Ministry of Foreign Relations and Culture, a position he was to resign in 1959 because of general dissatisfaction with government policy.

By 1960 Sábato was hard at work on the final draft of his greatest work to date, the novel *Sobre héroes y tumbas*. Actually the period of gestation of this masterpeice extends back to 1938 when sections of the novel were originally written for the unpublished work, "La fuente muda." Complex, overpowering, enigmatic, *Sobre héroes y tumbas* gives the reader a vision of Argentina, and especially of Buenos Aires, so broad in scope that only after numerous readings and much reflective meditation can one hope to begin to comprehend its total meaning. Sábato himself refuses to attempt a summary of his novel except to say that it is an attempt to describe the drama of human beings who have been born and who have suffered in "this anguished nation" (*Escritor*, p. 17). At the same time he presents a bit of the spiritual drama of every man—his search for the absolute and for eternity despite the frustrating and menacing presence of death as the negation of his search. Yet condemned as man is, Sábato sees a kind of absurd hope which allows him to continue. This oversimplification of the theme of *Sobre héroes y tumbas* will serve as an introduction to the systematic interpretation of the novel which will be undertaken later in this study.

If *El túnel* was to bring international recognition to its author, *Sobre héroes y tumbas* catapulted him into the very center of the sometimes tempestuous literary world. Commentaries and evaluations of his work are legion; the author is constantly sought for interviews, and his comments are read by an eager public. In an effort to answer the more significant questions most commonly put to him concerning his novels, Sábato prefaced his next collection of essays, *El escritor y sus fantasmas*, with some fifty pages of answers to these queries. This is followed by a rather cohesive statement on arts and letters in the present age of crisis, a kind of summary of his own work as it relates to the total perspective of current literature. The last section of his volume returns to the fragmentary style of his earlier essays, *Uno y el universo* and *Heterodoxia*, but the central theme of literary observations gives a certain unity lacking in the earlier works cited.

Sábato's name appears on another volume which appeared in 1964. It is a collection of essays called *Tango, Discusión y clave* (*Tango, Discussion and Key*) which Sábato assembled with the help of three young collaborators. The purpose of the volume is to analyze the tango from its origin to the present day using not only the opinions of the authors but also those of other commentators on the subject from André Gide to Jorge Luis Borges. Subsequent collections of Sábato's essays have appeared in recent years. Two of these collections, *Tres aproximaciones a la literatura de nuestro tiempo* (*Three Approaches to the Literature of Our Time*) and *Itinerario* (*Itinerary*) are in reality anthologies of essays previously published either in journals or in earlier volumes. In 1969 *La convulsión política y social de nuestro tiempo* (*The Political and Social Upheaval of Our Time*) was issued. Its alphabetical arrangement of contemporary ideas from Lenin to Henry Ford, from Picasso to Camus, and from Mao to Freud resembles the structure of *Uno y el universo* and the anthological nature of *Tango, Discusión y clave*.

Within all of Sábato's fiction and in certain of his essays the basic idea of a journey is present. This motif is announced in the preface of his first volume of essays, *Uno y el universo*, in which he embarks on a journey to distant lands in search of man and God only to return to the elusive search for himself, finally realizing that the universe is within him as it is within every other human being. While this idea is apparent in many of his other essays, it is in his first novel, *El túnel*, that the journey theme is next explored. The protagonist, a sometime painter named Juan Pablo Castel, takes the reader along with him on a trip which ends in the hermetic isolation of his own soul and ultimately in insanity. Sábato points out that in the case of Castel he is describing an extreme example of paranoia and isolation and that, at least from the vantage point of more than a decade of experience after writing his first novel, the exceedingly pessimistic conclusion is not to be taken as a definitive statement of his philosophy of life.

All four of the protagonists of *Sobre héroes y tumbas*, Sábato's gigantic second novel, embark on journeys of self-discovery. The dominant figure in the novel sets out on an obsessive quest for an answer to the problems which life has dealt him, and this leads him on a symbolic journey not unlike the one taken by Juan Pablo Castel. Other figures in this novel engage in a great deal of soul-searching which eventually leads them to a journey along the road to self-discovery. Not all of them achieve this goal, but it is significant to point out that one of the central figures of the second novel does overcome a series of overwhelming adversities and offers the reader—and Argentina as well for that matter—a message of hope and optimism after hundreds of pages of dense and crushing frustration.

This, then, is the chronology of the life of Ernesto Sábato, described in a recent study as a nervous, tense, somewhat arbitrary person but at the same time an individual with a generous heart.[6] In recent years he has served as a consultant to the López publishing company and has published articles and comments in various reviews in Argentina as well as in Peru, France, Cuba, Chile, and Mexico, and in 1962 he made an extended lecture tour in Europe. An interview in *Señales* announces plans for an essay dealing with the identification of the characteristics of a national literature and a third novel.[7] Although the former is the collection published by Aguilar in 1963 under the title *El escritor y sus fantasmas*, Sábato's ardent public is still eagerly awaiting the appearance of his next novel.

CHAPTER 2

Sábato the Essayist

A N evaluation of Ernesto Sábato's collections of essays leads
one to the conclusion that his production in this genre
is basically oriented toward the study of the human being
in an irrational and transitory universe. He is, in the words of
John Fred Petersen, a humanist.[1] A talent for essay writing
is evident in all of these collections, although it is apparent
that in the volumes of essays the results are uneven, occasionally leaving the reader confused by the encyclopedic
nature of certain collections while reaching the zenith of
lucidity and clarity in others.

If man is the protagonist of Sábato's essays, it is the rational
world of science which is the adversary. Granted that there
are numerous essays which deal with other subjects, it nevertheless remains that this central theme continues throughout
the essays and extends, as it were, into *El túnel* and *Sobre
héroes y tumbas*. At the same time, the critic is loath to divorce
the essay and the novel in the case of Sábato since the latter
frequently displays marked tendencies of the former. Even
a separate consideration of the two novels offers the critic
numerous problems due to the interweaving of themes. All
of Sábato's writings are therefore best considered as a unified
whole, but to simplify such an onerous task the textual divisions
into which Sábato casts his thoughts will be followed.

Thematically there are two general divisions into which fall
six of the collections of essays. The seventh, *El escritor y
sus fantasmas*, stands apart as a general summary of the
author's thoughts on the nature and purpose of literature.
At the same time Sábato answers a number of questions
concerning his own role as a literary artist. In consideration
of the fact that he feels that it is the prerogative of literature
to explore any and all aspects of man and his universe, this
volume may therefore be considered, at least tentatively, as
a definitive statement of his literary philosophy.

Three collections of essays deal specifically with the central theme of Sábato's literary production as outlined above. They are *Uno y el universo* (1945), *Hombres y engranajes* (1951), and *Heterodoxia* (1953). Three additional collections of essays, all of which appeared after the fall of Perón, deal more directly with Argentine themes but at the same time show a close spiritual relationship to the other essays. *El otro rostro del peronismo* and *El caso Sábato*, both of which appeared in 1956, are lucid commentaries on the tragic political dichotomy which existed for decades in Argentina and which was responsible for the chaotic national situation at the time they were published. *Tango, Discusión y clave* (1963) analyzes that "humble suburb of Argentine literature which is the tango." As in *El otro rostro del peronismo*, this volume makes a historical survey of the origin and development of the popular musical and dance form, but Sábato uses this vehicle to add numerous comments on a variety of other topics.

I *On Man and the Failure of Science*

When *Uno y el universo* first appeared, the intelligentsia of Argentina was unanimous in its recognition of Sábato as one of the brightest young figures on the literary horizon. Awarded a literary prize by the city of Buenos Aires, Sábato used this first volume to gain entry into the upper sphere of the River Plate world of letters. In later years critics examining this first volume in the light of Sábato's more mature efforts have concluded that it is highly imperfect as a cohesive statement or credo, a fact recognized by Sábato himself in his view of the book—one of tender irony—some eighteen years after its publication. Ostensibly it is an attempt to repudiate the world of science. Its publication came shortly after his year of disillusionment in Paris at the Curie Laboratory and his subsequent study at the Massachusetts Institute of Technology, yet it is replete with many of the very scientific notions he sought to repudiate.

Uno y el universo contains seventy-four entries listed in alphabetical order. They range in length from aphoristic statements of a line or two (Genghis Kant: A barbaric conquistador and a German philosopher) to statements on fascism, expansion of the universe, the future of barbarism, and

Surrealism which extend to more than ten pages. In the preface
the author affirms that the reflections which appear in the
volume are not the product of vague contemplation of the world
about him. Rather they are units of thought which he has
encountered along the road to self-discovery. Here then is
the key to *Uno y el universo* and to Sábato's career as a writer:
one seeks to know distant lands, man, nature, or perhaps even
God; later it becomes apparent that the phantom so assiduously
sought is one's own self. It is, in short, a journey into the
personal universe of Sábato on which the reader embarks,
and the seventy-four entries represent various stages in the
revelation of the personal philosophy of the man.

There are in this volume no pretensions of a philosophical
system implied; Sábato is not so dogmatic as to profess to be
the possessor of the only system of truth. Here as in the other
essays an attempt is made to reveal the author's personal
convictions, his universe. In the preface he makes an allusion
to his sojourn in the world of science which he now declares
a thing of the past, although such essays as those on the
expansion of the universe and Pythagoras belie the complete
divorce. In all fairness to Sábato, however, it must be pointed
out that throughout *Uno y el universo* he takes issue with the
scientific world, but remembering the fact that only a few years
before he had still held two professorships in physics, one
can still see the mind of the scientist behind these early essays.

The essays of this first collection have been divided into
eight categories: art and literature, education, history, philosophy, politics, religion, science and mathematics, and literary
style.[2] Needless to say, there is so much overlapping of theme
and content that many of the essays could just as easily be
placed in several categories. The alphabetical arrangement of
the entries leads to an almost complete loss of continuity,
but at least it is a kind of arrangement which permits one
to refer back to a previously stated idea. By far the largest
number of entries deals with art, including literary art and
style, and with science and mathematics.

In separate essays Sábato rejects the goal of automatism
of the Surrealists and "photographic" reproduction of the
external world advocated by nineteenth-century Realists.
The former when carried to its ultimate conclusion does not

invariably produce a thing of beauty, and the carbon-paper reproductions of the Realists are completely unnecessary. The latter are, in addition, as completely subjective as is any creative work. Sábato thereby provides a key to the subjective essays and novels he was to write after 1945. It is a subjective world that is described; the four protagonists of his novel, *Sobre héroes y tumbas*, all contain autobiographical characteristics. The universe for Sábato, then, is his own particular domain.

The very subjective values which Sábato assigns to art and letters are, because of their absence from pure science, the basis of his rejection of his years as a student and professor of physics and mathematics. There is, therefore, a close relationship between the central themes of *Uno y el universo*. Pure science disregards and rejects human and artistic emotions and sentiments and eliminates, as it were, the anguish one faces at the prospect of death. If science were the only world, it would be devoid of the illusory beauty and emotional satisfaction of painting, music, and literature. Sábato states that unless the alarming dominance of science is brought to a halt, the world will be transformed into a series of geometric curves, logarithms, Greek letters, triangles, and probability projections, and nothing more than this. A second key to the author's later writings is provided by this rejection of science. Within his personal philosophy nothing will be admitted which does not include human emotions and the element of subjectivity. The writer and the painter must view the world as they see and comprehend it without subjecting their vision to any set of preconceived scientific principles.

While Sábato's consideration of history in *Uno y el universo* is limited to certain observations concerning the distortion of facts through apocryphal additions and posterior reexamination, the germ of a later historical essay, *El otro rostro del peronismo*, may be found here. On the subject of politics Sábato is more extensive. Although his disenchantment with communism occurred some ten years earlier, his essay on socialism in this volume still supports numerous collective enterprises and group action against the dominating power of the machine age. The problem of fascism is considered in an

extensive essay of some fifteen pages. Rejecting the idea that
it is essentially a German and Italian phenomenon, he makes
a careful analysis of the social and economic conditions which
made such a political travesty possible. His conclusion is
that given the proper conditions, fascism is a latent movement
which could rear its head anywhere at any time. His analysis
of the conditions which caused the rise of fascism are again
reminiscent of his analysis of the rise of Peronism in the essay
previously mentioned.

The problem of religion and the existence of God has always
remained marginal in Sábato's essays and novels. Under the
essay on values it is pointed out that man is prone to attribute
to God his own ethical and esthetic prejudices. Does God
really exist? Sábato answers that if a census were taken of
the great minds of the world, a majority would answer in
the affirmative. As for Sábato, a relatively young man of
thirty-four when this volume was written, he finds equal
proof—really lack of proof—to support either viewpoint. In
an interview granted in 1962 in *Indice de artes y letras*, however,
Sábato indicates a move away from complete indecision on this
point when he affirms that he is not ready to reject that which
illustrious geniuses from Saint Augustine to Albert Schweitzer
have firmly believed.[3]

Uno y el universo presents no system of philosophy although
almost every one of the seventy-four essays could be classified as philosophical in nature. An underlying philosophical
theme, however, is the transitory nature of both man and his
universe. Sábato prefaced this volume with an epigraph taken
from André Gide's *Pages de Journal* in which the French
writer states that when three lines are sufficient to state a
point, he sees no reason to write a book or an article. Sábato
remained faithful to this principle, even reducing Gide's
three lines to one on some occasions. Although the lack of
continuity in the text detracts somewhat from its readability,
its importance as the compendium of a great variety of ideas
developed more fully in later works should never be overlooked.

A second collection of essays, *Heterodoxia*, is thematically
very similar to the first volume. *Heterodoxia* contains one
hundred and seventy-seven separate essays in one hundred
and twenty pages, whereas *Uno y el universo* extended to

two hundred and eleven pages with less than half as many entries. While it contains one essay which points out the vital necessity of heterodoxy, the book really contains two basic themes: a series of observations on the differences between masculinity and femininity; and a collection of observations on language, literary style, and literature. The title might have been more appropriate for the encyclopedic *Uno y el universo* where the variety of ideas and scope of presentation were considerably more ecumenical.

A four-line entry in *Uno y el universo* presents the theme of the first section of *Heterodoxia* in the following words: "There always will be a man who, although his house may be crumbling, will be worried about the Universe. There will always be a woman who, although the Universe may be crumbling, will be worried about her house" (*Uno*, p. 117). Sábato apparently felt that the idea expressed in this quotation was significant, for he chose to repeat it verbatim in *Heterodoxia*. This central theme of the dichotomy of the sexes is summarized in the following quotation: "Man shows a tendency toward the world of abstraction, of pure ideas of reason and logic. Woman adapts herself better to the world of the concrete, of adulterated ideas, of the irrational, of the intuitive" (*Heterodoxia*, p. 15). All of Sábato's additional comments on this subject are simply variations of this one central theme. He starts with an anatomical analysis of the sexes: Physically, spiritually, and mentally man projects his being while his companion acts as a receptacle, a point of union and fusion. Developing this theory to its ultimate conclusion, one sees man develop into the scientist, the philosopher, and the man of letters. Women too may reach a certain level of competency in science and letters, but Sábato cites the fact that none has achieved recognition as a philosopher, the highest stage of abstraction, as proof of his thesis.

Carrying his thesis another step, Sábato views the industrialization of the world as essentially a feminine activity in that it was the distaff side of primitive society which developed the first notions of agriculture, the domestication of animals, painting, medicine, the preparation and conservation of food, and the manufacture of artifacts. But as basic industry grew out of the domestic stage, it gradually became a masculine

activity what with the flowering of huge capitalistic enterprises
and the consequent abstraction of the industrial process.
A love for things on an abstract plane is a masculine trait,
while woman manifests her love for the immediate, tangible
surroundings of her home.

A series of comments on literature and style forms the
other corpus of ideas in this collection. There is no dividing
line between these ideas and those dealing with the differences
between the sexes. Both sets of comments are scattered throughout the book; however, the first section is more concerned
with the battle of the sexes and the second with literature.
Interpolated among these ideas are observations on the
subjectivity of history (an idea previously expressed in *Uno
y el universo*), observations on philosophical systems, and
comments on communism and capitalism. His observations
on the nature of language also fall into the general category
of literature.

By no means a purist in the matter of language and
literary style, Sábato rejects those who attempt to make
language conform to a dictionary or to the pronouncements
of an academy. His concept of two types of language—a
language of science and a language of life,—is an original
thesis reached in part because of his earlier contacts with the
world of science and subsequently with the world of art.
Ironically, he points out that the works of Shakespeare,
Cervantes, Dante, and Montaigne contain so many "errors"
because these authors did not have the benefit of an academy
dictionary. Likewise he takes Américo Castro to task for
stating that certain elements in Argentina are creating lin-
guistic anarchy, stating at the same time that the only
languages which are no longer anarchic are those which are
dead. Sábato's theories on language are very much in accord
with those of the structural linguists.

As a starting point for an analysis of the literary observations contained in *Heterodoxia*, one might consider the two
types of literature which Sábato sees as a result of the decay
of the modern world: literature of adventure and action
(Malraux, T. E. Lawrence, Saint Exupéry) and literature of
the ivory tower variety (Valéry, Borges). Action and contemplation are the two primordial forces behind these movements,

both of which seek their own particular kind of order in a chaotic world and at the same time a key to the enigma of existence. As a result, the contemporary novelist often disguises reality to achieve his ends. It should be emphasized that it is the contemporary *novel* which disguises reality since Sábato feels that the novel itself goes out in search of an author. A novelist should not write unless he is obsessed with and constantly pursued by the theme of his work. In the same breath he rejects detective stories as mere rational attempts at puzzle solving.

Perhaps the most valuable essay of all in this collection is that which deals with the Argentine novel. In defense of the novel of his country, Sábato answers the critics who affirm that a truly national novel has not yet been produced with the reply that Argentina is so complex a nation that a definition is highly elusive. The chaotic world of today is doubly chaotic in Argentina due to the fact that it is made up of an immigratory population. To describe the many nuances of spirit requires a series of literary works interpreting the decadent oligarchy, the fading gaucho, the *gringo* elements, and the cosmopolitan inhabitants of Buenos Aires.

Sábato decries the widespread opinions of Americans that the streets of Buenos Aires are populated with gauchos. He goes on to say that the literature of Argentina is urban, and even the pampa is described from the urban point of view. Immigration and industrialization have also contributed to the character of the novel. As a result the literati fall into three principal groups: the aristocratic class, the plebeian group, and those writers of the contemporary period like Sábato who seek a synthesis of these two extremes.

With these observations on the twentieth-century literary scene, Sábato closes *Heterodoxia*. Almost immediately after publication Victoria Ocampo's journal *Sur* reviewed the volume, and the critic, Alvaro Fernández Suárez, while finding certain valuable ideas within its pages, severely criticized Sábato for producing an orthodox book, lacking in originality and full of shortcomings.[4] A few months later Sábato answered these charges, also in *Sur*, and after admitting many of the weaknesses, indicated that he felt that there were certain positive contributions in *Heterodoxia*.[5] Among them were his

attempted synthesis of various theories on sex, his treatment
of the relations between author and literary work, and his
observation on language, the detective novel, the contemporary
novel in Argentina, and the works of Sartre. An inescapable
conclusion is that the volume has a certain value especially
in the area of literary interpretation. It does, however, suffer
when compared with *Hombres y engranajes*.

There is no doubt that *Hombres y engranajes* is Sábato's
most representative essay. Here is the best example of an
entire volume constructed around a central theme, man's
desperate struggle to realize his spiritual potential as an
alternative to the menacing fate of being a mere cog in the
gears of the mechanical age. The subtitle of the volume indicates that it is a study of money, reason, and the decay
of modern times. To reach these conclusions Sábato goes
back to the Middle Ages and the Renaissance for keys to the
understanding of the present age. Petersen summarized these
reflections in the following words:

> The guide-lines along which Sábato has conceptualized the world
> of the Middle Ages and its development into the Renaissance might
> be summarized—keeping in mind that his two previously stated key
> words are: reason and money—as a kind of circular series of inter-
> related antipathies leading from the world and man to Christianity,
> Humanism, Antiquity and Science. The lines of relationship, how-
> ever, are made less clear—even in the Renaissance—by man's
> instincts . . . and by the contributions of the Germanic peoples to
> Renaissance and later life. . . .[6]

As a result of these currents, modern man suddenly finds
himself in a kind of abstract world of reason and science,
the most notable example of which is the United States where
capitalism spawned cities from nothing. In the United States
Sábato sees an orientation toward functionalism and quantity
even to the point of numbering the streets of its great cities.
Assembly line industry—even assembly-line murders—have
relegated man to the position of a mere cog in the gears of
production. This kind of super state which is a result of
faith in science and technology is also apparent in the Soviet
Union as well as elsewhere in Europe, Asia, and Latin America.
The only difference between the capitalistic super state and

and the Communistic variety is that the latter only opposes the *use* of the machine for capitalistic ends; it in no way opposes the dominance of the machine itself. Furthermore, Sábato states that it is impossible to find any significant difference between state capitalism and state communism.

One of the first reactions to the power of science and technology was Romanticism. This reaction can be seen in the opposition of the individual to the human mass, the past to the future, the countryside to the city, and nature to the machine. Artistically, Romanticism ended in Surrealism; this according to Sábato, ultimately was its downfall as the Surrealists in their opposition to all rational forms of thinking in life and in government, were inevitably attracted to the Russian Revolution and thereby to Marxism. Neither Romanticism nor Marxism has successfully counteracted the headlong rush into a world of the mechanical robot, called the "Hombre–Cosa" by Sábato. Interestingly enough it was the scientists of the twentieth century, among them the creators of the atomic bomb, who first began to doubt the utility of their creations. In literature and philosophy there had been many a doubting soul—Pascal, William Blake, Dostoevsky, Baudelaire. Lautréamont, Kierkegaard, Nietzsche, and finally Franz Kafka, who Sábato feels expressed the sense of anguish of man in his dilemma better than anyone else. In the meantime man continued his bleak existence until such time as a general war would come along to free him from the routine. Paradoxically, Sábato feels that modern mechanized war with its numbered armies, divisions, and regiments, imposes even more routine than daily life. Guided by telephones and radios, the modern robots advance toward positions marked with letters and numbers. Then when some anonymous bullet fells him, he is buried in a geometrically arranged cemetery. Later one from among the multitude is removed to a symbolic tomb called the Tomb of the Unknown Soldier which for Sábato is a mere convention to designate the tomb of mechanized modern man, the tomb of the "Hombre–Cosa."

Sábato offers a third opposing force to these extreme consequences of mechanization in Existentialism, an evaluation and probing of the eternal problems of the meaning of life and death. This leads one to the final section of the essay

in which Sábato studies Existentialist literary production
as an answer to the problems previously outlined. This
attitude of investigation into the fundamental problems of
man's existence goes back, according to Sábato, to Dostoevsky's
Notes from Underground, from which he cites the following
passage: "But what can a decent man speak of with most pleasure? Answer: Of himself. Well, so I will talk about myself."[7]
With the exception of certain figures such as Dostoevsky,
most nineteenth-century novelists sought to paint esthetically
pleasing pictures of the "real" or rational world. It was an
outstanding century for the *nineteenth*-century novel, and
there is little difficulty in translating their plots to the motion-
picture screen. But in the present century there is no interest
in objective studies of reality. Today a tragic conception of
reality inspires a good deal of the literature produced, and the
most common themes are anguish, fear of death, lack of communication, madness, and suicide. The twentieth-century
novel is a tale told by an idiot, full of sound and fury.

In analyzing Existentialism, Sábato takes a wary look
at those like Sartre who reject the very existence of God.
Such an absurd total lack of hope in the future is a meaningless
philosophy for Sábato. As will be seen in *Sobre héroes y
tumbas*, the very fact that man continues to struggle within
his circle of operations and to produce works of beauty in
the middle of a hostile world is in itself a source of continued
hope. Existentialism seeks a conciliation between the objective and the subjective world, between the absolute and the
relative, and as a result of this attitude Sábato hopes to see
a synthesis of man and the community in which he lives.
As the late Jewish philosopher Martin Buber stated, indi-
vidualism disregards society, and collectivism refuses to
consider the individual. A dialogue between these two states
of being is Sábato's answer to the dilemma of man in a scientific
age; man with man, not man as a gear in a machine, is his
objective.

When viewed collectively, *Uno y el universo*, *Heterodoxia*,
and *Hombres y engranajes* offer a unified system of thought
on man, particularly Western man, as he faces a bleak and
unsympathetic world of reason. Except for the last volume
considered, this unified system is not apparent when reading

the individual collections. One must constantly reread and categorize some two hundred and fifty separate entries in the first two volumes, but in *Hombres y engranajes* an organized essay with four principal divisions makes for immediate comprehension of the themes. In *El otro rostro del peronismo*, *El caso Sábato*, and *Tango, Discusión y clave* Sábato followed the plan of organization of *Hombres y engranajes*. In each case these volumes are much shorter than the three already discussed, and an analysis of their contents is a less difficult task.

II *Argentina: Variations on a Theme*

The decade from 1945 to 1955 was one of the bitterest and most confusing in the turbulent history of Argentina. In this relatively short time Colonel Juan Domingo Perón and his ambitious, ruthless wife Eva Duarte rose to the highest level of Argentine politics, using the masses of unionized labor and the military as bases for their power. Although their careers were relatively brief—Eva died of cancer on July 26, 1952, and Perón was forced into exile by a military coup in 1955—they left an indelible mark on the nation they so completely dominated. The Perón era and the subsequent period of military rule after his defeat are the subjects of two additional essays to be considered in this section along with the more recent collection, *Tango, Discusión y clave*.

Sábato suffered greatly during the Perón dictatorship because he insisted on speaking out against the dictatorial suppression of the right to criticize and to differ with the national government on its basic policies regarding civil rights. As a result of his criticism he was dismissed in 1945 from his two professorships ostensibly for protesting the killing of a student in the streets of Buenos Aires during a student protest. Later he was condemned to two months in prison for supposed expressions of disrespect to the new regime. With such antecedents one would expect the volume, *El otro rostro del peronismo*, to be filled with bitter denunciations of the fallen dictator. Such is not the case. Rather, it is a study of the historic resentment that has existed in Argentina since the days of independence, first between the gaucho and the immigrant class of Buenos Aires, and later between the immigrants

themselves and the wealthy elite. Here again the reader is
reminded of the discrimination Sábato had experienced as
the son of Italian immigrants in the town of Rojas. It should
be pointed out, however, that during Sábato's childhood
the shift toward industrialization, particularly in the greater
Buenos Aires area, had brought about the second example
of rancor which he describes here as the struggle between
the immigrant class and the wealthy elite. In short, the historic
disregard for the rural and urban masses by the government
and the ruling classes produced a Pandora's box of social
and political ills which provided fertile ground for the rise
of an obscure colonel named Juan Domingo Perón who understood the masses and who opportunely took advantage of
their legitimate demands for social justice.

As a pretext for writing this volume, Sábato addresses
it as an open letter to one Mario Amadeo whose book, *Ayer, hoy
y mañana*, dealt with many of the same topics as *El otro rostro
del peronismo*. Ideologically, however, there are certain issues
in the current political and social scene of Argentina which
Sábato feels were either ignored or misunderstood by Amadeo;
hence the *raison d'être* of this open letter.

If Perón was an opportunist, his program, at least on paper,
presented the masses with such sufficiently defined goals that
they were ready to follow him blindly along the road to tyranny
and national degradation in much the same way as the German
and Italian masses in the 1930's followed leaders of a similar
orientation into a dehumanized state of animal barbarism.
As early as 1946 Sábato had detected those trends and had
proposed a popular movement which would oppose Perón but
at the same time offer the masses their due measure of liberty
and social justice, not mere social justice alone without the
necessary degree of liberty, which Perón offered.

The essay now moves into a more personal vein, and Sábato
describes reactions to the events of 1955 which led to Perón's
downfall with such fervor that for a time one has the sensation
that the essay has shifted into the field of fiction. On September
14, Sábato was in Tucumán to give a lecture. Because of the
tragic national situation his remarks were haphazard and
uninspired until someone asked him what he understood
Argentine national literature to be. Suddenly within him he

felt his repressed ideas rise up and come forth almost against his will. The national literature of Argentina, he said, should not be a showcase of gaucho costumes and picturesque regional speech but rather a vital new literature expressing the solitude, sadness, and desperation of the nation. A disguised literature of mores and customs was totally incapable of describing a nation lost in a tragic political carnival. He went on to say that he and many others were ashamed of being Argentine because of the events of the past decade, but all should recognize that every citizen of Argentina was in part responsible for the current situation; in every Argentine citizen there was and there is a fragment of Perón. At this point a number of people who held government posts rose in protest and left the lecture, but many remained to participate in the continued inquiry into these unpleasant realities.

The following day Sábato left Tucumán for Salta, and during the trip he studied the rugged countryside of the north. Was this dry, rugged pampa populated by taciturn Indians, this nation broken into infinite pieces the same one described by his elementary schoolteachers back in Rojas? Did the Indians of Salta, the gaucho of the north, and the aristocratic families of this northern province really have anything in common with the millions of immigrants and their descendants in the megalopolis of Buenos Aires?

Sábato remained for a number of days in Salta, and slowly answers to his questions came in the form of news broadcasts from the Puerto Belgrano naval base near Bahía Blanca and from the provincial capital of Córdoba. As Sábato and his friends hovered around the radio to hear every report of the victorious revolution against Perón, he realized that Argentina truly was one nation, a nation of more than twenty million heterogeneous souls sharing a common heritage and a foundation established on the heroes and tombs of past greatness. Here, then, is the rationale behind the title of Sábato's latest novel, *Sobre héroes y tumbas.* But while Sábato and his friends were celebrating the fall of Perón in a house in Salta, he noticed two Indian servants in the kitchen weeping quietly over their leader's defeat. It is this devotion to a tyrant which might just as easily have been translated to devotion for a just and democratic leader years ago that is the other face of Peronism. This legitimate spirit has been overlooked almost from the days of the Revolution of May in 1810, and until it is recognized, there can be no true synthesis of the various national groups.

As a conclusion to this essay Sábato offers a number of suggestions for resolving the crisis. In the first place it must be recognized that a number of positive contributions were made between the years 1943 and 1955. Although a demagogue was produced, at the same time a large segment of the population was brought for the first time into the political life of the nation. The middle class must be understood, and its leaders must realize the importance of their future role in history. Labor unions must be returned to the workers themselves to whom they legitimately belong. Vengeance and persecution must cease. (This last point is the basis for his next essay, *El caso Sábato.*) It must be recognized that everyone in the nation has shared the responsibility for recent events, and respect must be extended to both the Peronists and the anti-Peronists. Finally, and this is perhaps the most important suggestion of all, the orderly process of elections must begin so that the reins of government may be given to duly elected representatives of the nation as a whole. It was not until 1958 that the last suggestion was made operational with the election of Arturo Frondizi who at first glance seemed to be an ideal compromise candidate pleasing to a segment of the old Radical party as well as to the Peronist elements. Whether Frondizi's subsequent rejection of the latter and his ultimate removal from the presidency by the military forces were a result of his failure to follow the principles of reconciliation set forth by Sábato is a matter for future historians to judge.

Hardly had the ink dried on *El otro rostro del peronismo* when another volume of nine documents was published privately by a group of citizens aroused by the difficulties Sábato was having with the provisional government of General Aramburu because of his unwavering stand against the repressive tactics used by the government against its opponents. Always a champion of complete freedom of the press, Sábato was to experience a series of disagreements with the interventor assigned to the Empresa Haynes which published *Mundo Argentino*, the popular journal he edited in 1955. The

interventor, Colonel Julio César Merediz, specifically opposed
the mention in *Mundo Argentino* of certain cases of political
imprisonment and of torture suffered by opposition elements
in various regions of the nation. The first three documents of
this brief outline Sábato's categorical refusal to alter a single
statement in the articles as they were originally written, his
resignation from the directorship of *Mundo Argentino* as a
result of this uncompromising stand, and the subsequent
resignation of thirty-three of his collaborators in support of
his position.

The next four documents are a result of Sábato's participation in a round-table discussion broadcast nationally on
August 24, 1956. Having seen the avenue of expression offered
by *Mundo Argentino* closed in his face, Sábato used the
official radio network to express his horror and disillusionment
as he witnessed a return to torture and police brutality on
the part of the government. For his gratuitous remarks he
was called before the Minister of the Interior, Doctor Lanaburu,
to defend himself and was summarily suspended from the
national cultural organization which had sponsored the broadcast. The charges were that Sábato had acted purely as a
private citizen when in reality he was to have represented the
association. In addition, the charges of torture which he made
were not backed up by concrete evidence. The debate continued for several days in the newspapers of Buenos Aires,
first with Sábato's rejection of the charges and the subsequent
suspension of his membership followed by his own voluntary
separation from the movement.

As a result of these events Sábato decided to publish an
open letter to President Aramburu in the press of the capital,
but only *Democracia* chose to publish his message. In several
ways the letter to Aramburu repeats many of the opinions
stated earlier in *El otro rostro del peronismo*. Brief mention
is made of the historical background of the present situation,
and Sábato again points out certain positive contributions of
the Perón epoch. It is the loss of personal liberty and freedom
of expression, liberties still in doubt under the provisional
government, that Sábato decries. While there are still many
who have a certain measure of faith in Aramburu and his
government, Sábato points out that there is also doubt in many

circles. The reassuring words pronounced by Aramburu in a speech in San Luis are without positive action to support them, and it is action, not words, that the populace desires.

Sábato's letter, despite its limited circulation in *Democracia*, reached the president, and its writer was invited first to the Ministry of the Interior and the following day to the president's office to air his views. A series of nine recommendations, not unlike the recommendations which conclude *El otro rostro del peronismo*, were presented and accepted insofar as the president felt that they could be in view of the delicate political situation. In general, Sábato called for a lifting of restrictions on the press and of control of news releases. At the same time, he sought freedom for political prisoners and a return of the labor unions to some degree of normalcy. The fact that Aramburu attempted in good faith to follow the advice of Sábato must be considered a partial victory for the latter in his struggle for freedom of expression. Still there was much left to be done, and the very fact that a group of private citizens felt that the publication of these nine documents was necessary indicated that the solution to the problem of freedom of the press was not immediate. Aramburu did manage, however, to steer a course through the troubled political seas until such time as free elections could be held and a duly elected government could take office in 1958.

The third collection of essays in this group, *Tango, Discusión y clave*, would at first glance appear to be far removed from the themes of the first two collections studied. Such is not the case, however, for many of the same historical misunderstandings described in *El otro rostro del peronismo* and later in *El caso Sábato* enter into his analysis of this typical song of Buenos Aires.

There are, nevertheless, significant differences between this book and the first two already discussed. Only the first twenty-three pages of *Tango, Discusión y clave* were written by Sábato, the balance of the volume being a collection of various opinions concerning the tango written by a variety of contemporary writers. Following Sábato's opening remarks are some one hundred and thirty pages of commentaries on the origin, evolution, and literary importance of this art form. The volume concludes with a glossary of special idiomatic vocabulary found in the lines of the tango. These commentaries and the glossary are the work of Tabaré Di Paula, Noemí Lagos, and Tulio Pizzini, collaborators in this project who worked under Sábato's direction.

Sábato's thesis in the opening pages of this volume is that the tango is a result of the hybridization of the millions of immigrants who arrived on the shores of the Río de la Plata during a period of less than a hundred years. Earlier in various essays Sábato had mentioned the resentment and bitterness which this influx of foreigners caused. The artistic result of these feelings is the tango, a sad thought set to dance rhythm. In many ways it is similar to the hybridization which produced Negro folk music in the United States. Within the lines of the tango Sábato sees the tortured manifestation of inferiority of the immigrant and his burning desire for success in love as well as in other areas of his new life. The motive behind the tango is not pleasure but rather meditation on a melancholy existence together with a nostalgia for a distant homeland. In a sense the tango, according to Sábato, probes the metaphysical problems of an emerging nation composed of millions of heterogeneous inhabitants whose common geographical home is Buenos Aires.

Although the basic purposes are widely divergent, the same elements used to explain the tango were used in *El otro rostro del peronismo* to explain the origin of the political dichotomy of Argentina. These same elements appear briefly in the open letter to General Aramburu in *El caso Sábato*, thereby providing a kind of thematic unity for these three variations on a single theme. In an interview published in *Indice de artes y letras* Sábato affirms that his love for Argentina is so intense that he can only criticize its present condition for remedial purposes.[8] This he has done in all three of the essays considered in this section, and the results can only be interpreted to read that because of his criticisms he is one of the nation's greatest patriots in a century when national pride and confidence have all but disappeared from the Argentine scene.

III *The Diary of a Writer*

In many ways *El escritor y sus fantasmas* is a synthesis of the previous volumes of essays published by Sábato. It is, in the words of the author, a series of variations on a single theme, a theme that has obsessed him from the very moment he began to write: Why and how does one write prose fiction? These notes and reflections, expanded here into a lengthy essay, form what Sábato calls a personal diary, something more like a confidential letter to a close friend than a book for the general public. At the same time, Sábato seeks to clarify for himself these vague intuitions concerning his own literary life, hoping that this process of self-analysis will also aid the young writer seeking to identify himself in the literary world and the literary critic "who explains to us how and why we should write."

Owing to its synthetic nature, this volume of essays contains a great deal of material either taken directly from previous essays or abstracted and revised from these same sources. This is especially true of the second and third sections of the book, which deal with art and letters in their present critical state. The first section of the collection contains replies to the fifty-two questions most frequently put to Sábato regarding his literary production and the motives behind it. The reader is presented with a rich literary autobiography containing occasional glimpses of events in the author's life which are related directly to his novels and essays. His experiences as a child in Rojas, as an adolescent student in La Plata, and as a confused young scientist in Paris and in Cambridge, Massachusetts, are graphically related in some of the more personal entries in the volume. Next he moves into a series of questions concerning *El túnel* and *Sobre héroes y tumbas*, the answers to which will be considered in the next four chapters of the present study. In the same section he answers questions concerning the methods he employs in writing novels. Based on his replies to these questions, one may conclude that writing is both physical and mental torture for Sábato, an activity which he cultivates "so as not to die of sadness in this distressed nation." Additional commentaries in this first section of *El escritor y sus fantasmas* seek to define the role and purpose of Argentine literature and to explain the nature of the twentieth-century Florida-Boedo split. Most of the ideas set forth in these passages appeared earlier in *Heterodoxia* and in the section from *El otro rostro del peronismo* in which he recalls his remarks on the meaning of Argentine national literature made in a speech delivered in Tucumán shortly before the fall of Perón. The positive contribution of the first section of *El escritor y sus fantasmas*, apart from the many personal elements revealed for the first time, is the collection in one place of Sábato's widespread commentaries on his own work and on Argentine letters in general.

In the second section Sábato cogently defines the present crisis through which man is passing and describes the literature which results from the basic conflict between a mechanized society and the individual. One is reminded almost immediately of *Hombres y engranajes*, which develops the same thesis. There are, indeed, long passages which Sábato lifted verbatim from this previous collection of essays. Inescapably he arrives at the same conclusions: the long historical process beginning in the Renaissance has resulted in a mechanized society against which man has rebelled through successive periods of Romanticism, Marxism, and Existentialism. The perennial themes of solitude, the absurdity of death, and the delicate balance between hope and desperation have acquired new relevance in the chaotic twentieth century. As Sábato sees it, the only solution to these problems is a highly personal one, an attitude which brought down the wrath of leftist critics on *El escritor y sus fantasmas*. His defense of the artist in his search for a profound personal solution to his anguish was not in line with Marxist collective realism any more than was his defense of Western literature compatibile with the superficial propagandistic lines that flowed from leftist pens. But not being one to compromise on vital issues, Sábato has remained firm in his disagreement with the leftist press just as he was intransigent in the controversy over freedom of the press with the provisional government of Aramburu.

In the review of *El escritor y sus fantasmas* published in *La Nación* it is pointed out that the third section of the collection lacks the cohesion of the first two sections.[9] These variations on the theme of contemporary literature offer much the same miscellany found earlier in *Uno y el universo* and *Heterodoxia*. There are one hundred and sixty-seven entries in this last section which runs to some one hundred and seventy pages. The second edition, published in 1965, contains an additional article on abstract art reprinted from a 1956 issue

of the Cuban journal, *Ciclón*. This third section runs the entire
gamut of literary topics from French Realism and Naturalism
to Borges and Henry Miller. The multiplicity of this section,
in which many of the entries are repeated from earlier essays,
prevents a detailed analysis of contents. If one can draw a
conclusion after reading these one hundred and sixty-seven
entries, it would be that the contemporary novel has as its
function the re-establishment of man as the focus of reality.
This section would clearly establish Sábato in the stream of
Existentialism if such an evaluation were still necessary.

In sum, *El escritor y sus fantasmas* may be considered a
key to the two novels which Sábato has produced. In it he
attempts to answer many of the most puzzling problems which
El túnel and *Sobre héroes y tumbas* have created in the literary
world, although at times Sábato himself throws up his hands in
despair at his inability to explain his own creations. His
own characters at times seem to go out in search of an author
to immortalize them, and Sábato views himself as an agent in
the creative process rather than a producer. He does, however,
correct a number of critical misinterpretations of his novels
and provide a means of understanding many enigmatic passages. Frequent references to this first section of *El escritor y
sus fantasmas* will therefore be made in the next four chapters
of the present study in which an analysis of Sábato's two
novels is essayed.

CHAPTER 3

The Defeat of Reason

CONSIDERING the great complexity of *El túnel*, one is somewhat surprised by the fact that the first line and a half reveals the essence of the novel's action: "I am Juan Pablo Castel, the painter who killed María Iribarne; that should be e-nough." One cannot escape from the aura of mystery and reader intrigue which the opening lines cast. An alternate translation of the opening clause more clearly demonstrates the subtle qualities of the original Spanish: "It is probably enough to say that I am Juan Pablo Castel...." Immediately the reader is confronted by a myriad of unanswered questions, and his only recourse is to read ahead in an attempt to answer them. No, it *is not* enough to say that the writer is Juan Pablo Castel; and who is María Iribarne, the woman whom he killed? Is it not presumptuous to speak of murder in such a matter-of-fact fashion? How could it be enough to stop after the first sentence? Castel fortunately continues the monologue, thereby answering some but by no means all of the enigmatic uncer-tainties with which he has confronted his readers.

As the plot gradually unfolds one is struck by its simplicity; it can be reduced to the tale of a misunderstood painter who enters into an illicit affair with the wife of a wealthy blind man, an affair which when frustrated by the lovers' inability to find a common basis for communication leads to murder. Although the action itself offers few complexities, the philosophic over-tones of the novel are such that the reader never quite escapes from the chaotic labyrinth into which Castel leads him.

Castel first met María in 1946 at an exhibition of his paint-ings held in the Salón de Primavera. One of his most important works, and in many ways a key to the novel, was a painting called "Maternidad." The central figures of a mother and her child were what called the attention of the critics and of all the viewers of the painting except one, María. In the upper left corner was painted a small window through which one

could see a small, remote scene of a woman on a lonely beach
looking out at the sea as if awaiting a distant, faint call. The
scene suggested to Castel poignant, absolute solitude. To
María Iribarne Hunter it must have suggested the same thing,
for her attention was fixed on the same minuscular scene for
a long period. Castel was positive that at last he had communi-
cated his inner feeling to another human being, but she was
now gone, lost among the anonymous millions of Buenos Aires.

A whole series of themes and character revelations begins
to emerge. The only difficulty is that the reader has no recourse but to accept all the facts in the case as they filter
through the mind of a madman, for by now it is relatively
certain that Castel is some sort of an idiot and that his tale
is one of sound and fury. His pursuit of María through the
streets of Buenos Aires is frustrating, for he has absolutely
no clues as to her identity or her center of activity. Their subsequent meeting and the tempestuous encounters which
follow—first in the Plaza San Martín, then in La Recoleta,
and finally in Castel's studio—run the entire emotional gamut
from tender moments of whispered love to violent scenes of
anguish and total absence of communication. By the time
the affair has extended to several weeks, the tormented nature
of Castel's personality is well developed. María, however,
remains at least a partial enigma for the reader as well as for
Castel. Her rather reserved mood and strange, penetrating
expression during the first interview are probably due to the
abrupt manner by which Castel approaches her. The intense,
burning questions he puts to her are either unanswered or
hesitatingly answered with a word or a phrase as if to indicate
María's reluctance to give of herself in any way to this strange
artist. The fact that Castel is a painter of some importance
while María is an unknown figure further increases the abyss
between them.

Castel does, however, succeed in establishing a tenuous
bridge between them based on feelings of mutual comprehension
of the solitude and spiritual isolation apparent in the window
scene. Despite María's protest that she always does harm to
all who come near her, Castel succeeds in arranging a second
interview. At this point a series of events begins to unfold
which only serve to cloud the picture of María's personality

that has begun to form. Her abrupt departure for the country, following the confirmation of their second date in a strained and somewhat enigmatic telephone conversation, serves to heighten Castel's despair and to draw him into an ever greater mystery. Before her departure she writes Castel a note which she leaves in the hands of her husband, Allende, thereby bringing about a face-to-face meeting of the two. One has the feeling that María desired this confrontation and used the letter as a ruse to effect it. Upon arriving at María's home, a comfortable apartment of Posadas Street, he is ushered into the library where bookshelves containing abnormally large volumes fill every available space from floor to ceiling. Suddenly Castel has the impression that someone is watching him from behind, and he turns to meet the blind stare of Allende's eyes.

At this point Sábato introduces one the the central themes of his two novels, a theme which is to occupy the entire third section of *Sobre héroes y tumbas*. For Sábato as well as for Castel the world of the blind is a kind of subworld which is both intriguing and ominous at the same time. Allende is cordial enough to the visitor whom he knows only as a friend of María, but Castel's discomfort in this strange situation is heightened by the unexpected discovery of her husband's blindness. The contents of the letter—one line stating "I am also thinking about you"—do not seem to be important enough to occasion Castel's trip across the city to receive it, that is, unless María has contrived the whole incident to bring about his encounter with her husband. Other facts about her, however, do emerge from the encounter: María always uses her maiden name, Iribarne; Allende's surname is Hunter, and it is a cousin of his with the same surname whom María is visiting on the family ranch. Hunter, the cousin, is a woman-crazy cynic well known in certain circles of Buenos Aires society, and the disclosure of María's visit to his ranch can only cause uneasiness in Castel's mind.

The stage has been set for the rest of the action in the novel. Again it must be pointed out that the action is all internal in that it flows through the tormented mind of Castel who relates a series of meetings with María punctuated by periodic unexpected journeys to visit her cousin Hunter. These absences only serve to accentuate Castel's anguish, for he suspects—and not without reason—that María and Hunter are lovers. Other elements adroitly used by Sabáto to complete the picture include an exchange of letters between María and Castel during the periods of her absence from Buenos Aires and a series of dreams which torment the painter's restless nights.

Viewed as a whole, *El túnel* is a desperate effort on the part of Juan Pablo Castel to communicate with another being, equally free and with a mind and spirit similar to his own. This theory has been analyzed in the subsequent volume of essays, *Heterodoxia*, in which this type of communication is offered as the only means of escaping from abject solitude and isolation.[1] Castel believes that physical union was the guarantee of true love and hence the bridge on which the two of them might meet and communicate. His subsequent disillusion with sex is described in the following terms:

> I will say right away that this was another of my many ingenuous ideas, one of those naivetés which surely made María smile behind my back. Far from reassuring me, our physical relations upset me still more, brought new and tormenting doubts, painful scenes of misunderstanding, cruel experiments with María. The hours we spent in the studio are hours I shall never forget. My feelings during this whole time ranged from the purest love to the most unbridled hatred because of María's contradictoriness and incomprehensible attitudes. (*Outsider*, p. 81)

Castel's frustration and anguish are increased by María's failure to answer questions which torment his mind: Why does she continue to use her maiden name? Why did she marry Allende? Do they have physical relations? What does she see in Hunter? Does she really love Castel or Allende or Hunter? As a result of the torment which these unanswered questions occasion, Castel gradually withdraws more completely into the tunnel of absolute isolation from the exterior world. The reader, too, is forced to enter the tunnel and view the exterior world through the eyes of his one and only guide. Castel takes the reader into his confidence and tells of his suicidal inclination, halted only by the prospect of later awakening in absolute nothingness, and revealing at the same time a plan which will terminate in María's death.

The foreboding nature of the plan developing in Castel's mind is announced by the statement that "the days that preceded María's death were the most horrible of my life" (*Outsider*, p. 140). Here one sees the last stages in the destruction of a rational mind as Castel flits from one frantic course to another in a vain attempt to find a measure of reason behind the conflicting events with which he is confronted. The state of confusion and disorder within him—within his tunnel— is best observed in a letter he writes to María, who is still at Hunter's ranch. Almost every line of the letter is rewritten two or three times in an effort to clarify to her the reasons for his accusations.

A hurried telephone call to María asking her forgiveness for the brutality of the letter results in his ending the conversation shouting insults far more violent than the contents of the letter itself. Completely disoriented, he begins making the rounds of the bars along the river front and finally returns to his studio with a prostitute. This secondary incident develops further the twisted concepts in his mind. Noting an expression of feigned pleasure on the prostitute's face, he recalls a similar expression on María's during a moment of passion: the prostitute pretends that she was experiencing pleasure; María also pretended the same thing; María is a prostitute.

The final scenes of the novel unfold with dizzy rapidity. Castel first goes to his studio and destroys his paintings, including the one with the window scene which first brought him together with María. He thereby destroys the tenuous bridge by which he hoped to establish communication with her just as she has destroyed the last hope of communication by allowing him to drift alone while she remained at the ranch. In a borrowed automobile Castel rushes down the Mar del Plata highway toward Hunter's ranch and his last rendezvous with María. Arriving shortly after the dinner hour, Castel quietly awaits the hour when the entire household will have retired. The seemingly interminable delay allows him to reminisce and formulate certain conclusions regarding their relationship. His original thesis was that he and María had both been living in parallel tunnels like twin spirits sharing the same historical epoch. Finally their spirits were to meet in a converging of the tunnels brought about by the window scene in "Maternidad". Now he realizes that this dream of union, of communication, was only a foolish illusion. In reality there always was only one tunnel, Castel's, and María out of curiosity had approached its strange windows to observe the lonely, tormented creature who had spent his childhood, youth, and adulthood in this endless corridor.

The anguish of the moment is heightened when Castel observes Hunter and María walking over the grounds of the estate after dinner. Then he witnesses a final incident which is to cement the feeling of infinite loneliness in his soul: María and Hunter retire to the same bedroom. Stunned and totally confounded, Castel stands outside the house through a violent storm until at last a light goes on in María's bedroom. Quickly he climbs to the upper story by means of a window grille, walks along the terrace, and enters her bedroom. With her huge, hallucinated eyes she asks him as he approaches her bed, "What are you going to do, Juan Pablo?" He replies, "I have to kill you María. You have left me alone" (*Outsider*, p. 174). Sobbing, he plunges a knife into her breast; then with a sudden fury he withdraws it and drives it repeatedly into her body.

Madly Castel returns to Buenos Aires and rushes to María's house where he confronts Allende with the announcement that María was Hunter's mistress, his mistress, and the mistress of many others, but that her days of deception are over. The blind husband screams at him that he is a fool as he runs from the house to turn himself in at the police station. From the window of his cell he watches the dawn of a new day and ponders the thought of men and women resuming the activities of their daily routine. But for Castel the black cavern within him seems to be growing bigger and bigger.

Sábato's original intention in writing *El túnel* was to present the history of a painter who went crazy when he discovered that he was unable to communicate with anyone, even with the woman who seemed to understand him through his painting. As the writing of the novel proceded, Sábato reports that he was perplexed by the unconscious changes which took place in the direction and emphasis of the thematic corpus (*Escritor*, pp. 13-14). The most important of these changes was the increasing importance which jealousy and physical possession gradually assumed. At times these digressions and new directions did not please the author, but he soon came to realize that in a way he had been relegated to the role of an intermediary between the reader and the world of fiction. The metaphysical world therefore transforms itself into a tale of passion and crime in which Castel attempts to possess María by means of sex. This, Sábato believes, is an impossible task. In sum, it may be pointed out that here physical sex bears a close relationship to violence, torture, metaphysical anguish, and therefore to death. Sábato views the final crime in *El túnel* as Castel's last attempt to "eternize" María, although at the same time he recognizes that it is probably Castel's last attempt at complete possession (*Escritor*, pp. 15-16). In any case, it is not completely a coincidence that the weapon is a knife plunged repeatedly into her body.

Although certain critics have classified *El túnel* as a work containing many aspects of detective fiction, such a classification is both inaccurate and unfair to an author who has openly rejected this genre as mere puzzle-solving on paper. Petersen views the novel as a statement on the isolation of modern man, a situation created by a long series of factors and forces resulting from the interaction of historical, religious, social, scientific, and cultural phenomena.[2] It becomes, therefore, a fictionalized statement of the theses set forth in the essay *Hombres y engranajes*. Castel as the protagonist is ensnared in the web of a world built upon reason, and his attempts to extricate himself from this entrapment only serve to draw him deeper into his corridor of despair. The end result is the destruction of María, the catalyst in this whole process, and the total physical and spiritual isolation of Castel.

The central symbol in the novel is the window scene in the upper left corner of the painting, "Maternidad." It has already been pointed out that for Castel this scene was the essence, so to speak, of the message he sought to convey. It suggested, in his opinion, a poignant and absolute loneliness. But the reference to motherhood in the title of the painting provides another key to his personality. The sea itself is a maternal symbol, and during Castel's first visit to María at Hunter's ranch there is evidence that she is a mother symbol for Castel as she caresses his face while they relive the scene in his painting. One must therefore consider the painting, "Maternidad," in its totality, for in the final analysis Castel is unable to divorce Oedipal tendencies in his relationship with María from the abject solitude suggested by the window scene. There is, of course, a great deal of maternal symbolism in the name María, and the juxtaposition of the roles of mother and lover lead to a type of philosophic incest. This star-crossed relationship is doomed to failure from the very beginning; María too is forced to enter Castel's tunnel, where she reaps the bitter harvest sown in the barrenness of her lover's soul. After María's murder Castel reaches the end of his tunnel, but the terminus is not a door but another window. His isolation and confinement are complete; Castel is able to view a small portion of the exterior world through the small window of his jail cell. He is able to ponder the last mad events before his confinement and Allende's subsequent suicide after María's death. But Castel is sure that the doctors who are observing him are laughing behind his back just as he suspected that they laughed during the trial when he attempted to explain the scene of the window. The only person who understood his painting is now dead, and the walls of this inner hell seal him tighter day by day.

Viewed as a statement of total isolation, *El túnel* is in the mainstream of twentieth-century Existentialism. Both Castel and Sábato seem to fit the category of the nonatheistic Existentialist. In *Hombres y engranajes* Sábato took a wary view of Sartre's rejection of the existence of God, and Castel states that Christ is "the being for whom I have felt and even today feel the deepest reverence. . . ." (*Outsider*, p. 6). At the same time, in *El túnel* one can see at almost every turn the Existentialist view of the absurdity of the world and the resulting withdrawal of the Existentialist protagonist into total isolation reminiscent of the idea of a hermetic existence as seen in Sartre's *Huis clos*. Sábato never reaches the depths of Sartrian despair which he finds absurd in itself, and he always sees a glimmer of hope—although only a glimmer— to urge mankind forward and to save it from total anguish. "Anyway, I can paint. . . ."Juan Pablo Castel concludes. Although there are many ways in which Sábato departs from a rigid Sartrian Existentialism, there is evidence in the fact that María is a reader of Sartre that he at least finds a certain brotherhood of anguish in the French novelist. Castel's insistence on the use of the name "Juan Pablo" may also be an indirect reference to Jean-Paul Sartre.

A comparison of the opening lines of *El túnel* with those of other contemporary Spanish American writers shows that Sábato falls into the category of magical Realism as defined and described by Angel Flores.[3] Magical Realism is basically the art of surprises, seeking from the very first line to throw the reader into a timeless flux or into an unconceivable situation saturated with dramatic suspense. This technique is readily observable in *L'Etranger* of Albert Camus and in various opening lines of Franz Kafka. Compare "It is probably enough to say that I am Juan Pablo Castel . . . ." with Camus's opening lines: "Mother died today. Or maybe, yesterday; I can't be sure." Both novels are written in a matter-of-fact style in the first person, and each is related after the occurrence of the murder. As pointed out by Petersen, both books may be considered statements on the indifference of the world to the individual, with Camus's work emphasizing the apathetic surroundings while Sábato paints a central figure oblivious to everything beyond his own ego.[4]

There are even closer ties between Juan Pablo Castel and Gregor Samsa, the protagonist of Kafka's *The Metamorphosis*. Kafka transports the reader into a world of his own invention as the story opens: "As Gregor Samsa awoke one morning from a troubled dream, he found himself changed in his bed to some monstrous kind of vermin." His monstrous nature is not unlike the deformed personality of Castel; both are unable to direct or to control their abnormal development, and both drop from the "real" world for all practical purposes. The set of circumstances surrounding each narrative is not a set of conjectures; the reader and the other characters accept it as an almost normal event, and the narrative continues on this magical foundation. The world of reason is therefore challenged and refuted from the very opening. Never is there an attempt to reach a level of clarity and explanation. Rather, the end result is one of ambiguity, for Kafka and Sábato both view the world as an enigmatic perplexity in which reason

fails to provide a key to its comprehension. Both works end
on an indifferent note: Samsa's corpse is swept up by the char-
woman, and Castel is isolated physically and spiritually from
the outside world.

In *Hombres y engranajes* Sábato traces this current of
introspection so apparent in *El túnel* back to the works of
Fyodor Dostoevsky, especially to his *Notes from Underground*.
Contemporary literature is, according to Sábato, a synthesis
of the subjective and the objective worlds in an effort to
interpret the crisis of twentieth-century life; this preoccupation
began with Dostoevsky and is evident in Marcel Proust,
Virginia Woolf, James Joyce, William Faulkner, and Franz
Kafka. Sábato would, of course, place himself in this same
current of writers who frequently describe the world through
the eyes of a disturbed protagonist. To emphasize this point
of view it is not uncommon to present the narrative in the
first person. Camus does this in *L'Etranger*; it is a technique
frequently employed by Faulkner and Dostoevsky. Sábato
reports that he spent a long time in choosing the person who
would narrate *El túnel* (*Escritor*, pp. 14-15). His final election
of the first person was brought about by his decision that the
process by which Castel gradually moved into a state of
delirium climaxed by the murder of María would be more
effective if described by the protagonist himself. Sábato
hoped thereby to permit the reader to experience the sensations which brought about the madness of Castel and to
give one the impression that he was in a way Castel's alter
ego. As the reader enters the soul of the protagonist, he inevitably reaches the point of questioning the reasons behind the
latter's existence in a corner of space and time surrounded,
as it were, by the infinite and constantly threatened by
death. His first thought is to communicate with another
doomed being by establishing tenuous bridges from one soul
to another in an attempt to initiate a dialogue. Castel sought
this very thing using the scene in his painting as the bridge,
but his was an extreme case of the very absence of the ability
to communicate. Such a case is not to be interpreted as a
normal situation, for Sábato deliberately sought to create
such an extreme situation to present his basic thesis. In contemporary fiction it is common to use these extreme forms

of psychic abnormality to state the case in point, and Juan Pablo Castel is no exception.

In his study of *El túnel*, Myron I. Lichtblau finds a number of picaresque characteristics which would relate the novel to one of the first novelistic genres cultivated in the Hispanic world.[5] The candid and direct nature of the narrative is not dissimilar to the picaresque novel, and in *El túnel* there is a mixture of perversity, roguery, and a certain maliciousness which recalls the tales of Lazarillo de Tormes vintage. There are, however, many similarities between Sábato's work and the novels of contemporary Spanish *Tremendismo*, a movement which seeks to accentuate the most depraved passions of mankind and the most disagreeable, cruel, and violent aspects of life by means of caricature and exaggeration. Its basic ingredients are Realism and spiritual anguish; secondary manifestations include violence, murder, horror, defeat, and cruelty. It is at once apparent that *El túnel* includes most of these elements, but its special form of Realism is not the type found in the *Tremendista* novel as practiced by Camilo José Cela in *La familia de Pascual Duarte*. Pascual Duarte and Juan Pablo Castel both face a cruel, indifferent world, but in the case of the former the author's principal intention is to shock the reader's sensibilities with the violent reality of contemporary Spanish life. Sábato's purpose is quite different; the exterior world in its indifference produces a twisted, tormented inner world in the mind of Castel into whose corners the reader is gradually introduced. Both novels end on a note of despair, but in the case of Sábato it is a philosophical state of desperation brought about by the breakdown of abstract reason. Cela accomplishes a similar level of hopelessness but uses physical phenomena as catalytic agents in the process.

Temporal and spatial considerations in *El túnel* closely parallel the subjectivity of Juan Pablo Castel and reflect the fluctuations of his mental and physical patterns of behavior.[6] In certain passages, time and space both assume static-like qualities and sink into a meaningless, unimportant role. This is most evident as Castel engages in long mental soliloquies about his relationship with María. He begins to weigh one possibility against another, gradually entering a kind of psychic reality in which conventional time-and-space rela-

tionships disappear. The following passage describing Castel's
vigil outside Hunter's house just prior to María's murder
clearly demonstrates his rejection of conventional time:

> The wait was interminable. I don't know how much time passed
> by the clock, that anonymous, universal time of clocks, which is
> alien to our feelings, our fate, the flowering or the shattering of love,
> the waiting for a death. But by my own time it was a vast and com-
> plicated span, full of things and turnings back, a river dark and tu-
> multuous at times, and at times strangely calm and almost like a
> still, unending sea, where María and I stood face to face, gazing at
> each other in rapture. (*Outsider*, p. 168)

An earlier passage describing Castel's first visit to Hunter's
ranch shows his lack of interest in his physical surroundings.
Shortly after his arrival Hunter takes him into the house to
the room he is to have. While going upstairs, Hunter explains
something of the history of the house to which Castel reacts,
"And what's that to me?" (*Outsider*, p. 113). His mental
orientation throughout the novel is directed toward the creation
of his own inner world, and he therefore demonstrates an inability to receive images from outer reality and to integrate
them into his personality. His attitude can best be described
as one of indifference to time and space when these manifestations of reality seem unimportant to him.

On other occasions, especially when his natural surroundings
parallel the violent emotions within him or when a confrontation with some aspect of the exterior world is imminent, the
time-space phenomena assume a level of importance com-
mensurate with their relationship to Castel's mood or course
of action. Frequently these moods are directly related to the
window scene of his painting, "Maternidad." For example,
the date and place of its exposition are clearly stated as are
its details of composition. During Castel's first visit to Hunter's
estate he and María relive the scene in objective detail. The
final destruction of the painting, in a way symbolic of the
impending mutilation of María, is recounted as each shred of
canvas falls to the floor. Finally, the scene from Castel's
jail cell at the end of the novel is one of objective reality as
he witnesses the birth of a new day and thinks of the men and
women in the external world having breakfast, going to the

office, reading the morning paper, feeding the children or the cat, or discussing the movie of the preceding night. All of these references to the window scene are closely related to his attempt to bridge the abyss, so to speak, and to communicate with another being. Although this is never possible, it is not because Castel does not ardently want to communicate and establish a bridge with the world outside of his inner reality.

Sábato's treatment of time also changes as the inevitable conflict between Castel and the exterior world approaches its climax with the murder of María. A veritable timetable of murder is unfolded: "It was six in the afternoon. I figured that with Mapelli's car I could make it in four hours, so I would be there by ten" (*Outsider*, p. 166). Castel continues by identifying the highway by which he left Buenos Aires and by indicating his speed as one hundred and thirty kilometers an hour. At a quarter past ten he reaches Hunter's ranch at which time the interminable wait for María to retire begins. With precise detail he observes the lights go on in Hunter's bedroom, but María's bedroom remains in darkness. His suspicions about their relationship are confirmed. Now the action begins to follow a rapid pace as María is murdered and Castel rushes back to Buenos Aires, arriving "at four or five o'clock in the morning." After the confrontation with Allende, Castel gives himself up at the police station. It is almost six o'clock.

Thus, for a period of twelve hours almost every incident in Castel's life is recorded by the hour and the minute. As in the case of the window scene, the protagonist is seeking to establish rapport with something outside himself; it is his last valiant effort to possess María, but it is only a momentary possession before he must again retreat into his inner self, where time and space lose their coherent forms. One may, therefore, conclude that temporal and spatial treatment in *El túnel* is an extention of the psychic condition of the protagonist and that the fluctuations observable in these two areas reflect his efforts to extricate himself from his own inner reality.

A series of three dreams also indicates the nature of one segment of Castel's mentality, his subconscious mind. In the first two dreams the central figure is a house which in one

way or another comes to represent María. In the first dream
Castel finds himself in a vaguely familiar house which in many
ways reminds himself of a house known in his childhood.
Others are present, and they seem to be ridiculing him in
some way. Nevertheless the house recalls his adolescent
awakening to the first currents of physical love while at the
same time creating feelings of fear and joy. When he awakes,
he realizes that his dream house is María, and the adolescent
maternal instincts only confirm the Oedipal tendencies previously discussed.

The second dream is far more violent than the first and
occurs after their relationship has entered a dubious stage with
Castel's confronting María with the suspicion that she is
deceiving Allende as well as himself. In the dream he and a
number of others were invited to the home of a gentleman.
Castel was the first arrival, and he immediately sensed that
he had fallen into a trap. Frantically he sought to escape,
but without success. Slowly his host began to change him into
a bird of human size, beginning with his feet and ending with
a monstrous head. His only hope was that his friends would
arrive and somehow break the magic spell. When they did
come, however, they failed to notice his transformation; even
the desperate screech of his voice was completely ignored.
Suddenly he realized that nobody would ever know that he
had been transformed into a bird.

Again the house represents María or at least the relationship
between him and María. The host is a representation of the
blind Allende who welcomed Castel into his home. It is possible to relate Castel's transformation into a monstrous bird
to his mental anguish and spiritual transformation upon
discovering on his first visit to María's house that she is
married to the blind Allende. Sábato later confessed in *El
escritor y sus fantasmas* that he personally feels a strange and
ambiguous feeling in the presence of the blind, and the transformation of Allende into the wizard of the dream is a logical
step. Perhaps in the second dream more than anywhere else
in the novel does one see the relationship between Castel and
Kafka's Gregor Samsa. Both are mysteriously converted into
monsters, and the world is oblivious to their fate as they

desperately seek to communicate their misfortune to those about them.

The third dream is only a sketch of Castel seated in a dark, empty room while Hunter and María look at each other in the background with an expression of diabolical irony. Occurring after his visit to the ranch and the confirmation of his feelings about them, this dream is a reflection of his mental state at a time when his anguish has neared the breaking point. The empty room is but another device which Sábato uses to describe Castel's tunnel and the complete void which fills his soul.

symbol

One cannot deny the importance of *El túnel* as a kind of central depository of all the themes found in Sábato's essays and in the monumental *Sobre héroes y tumbas*. The almost total isolation of man in a world dominated by science and reason is the most important of these themes, but at the same time the reader also sees the inability of man to communicate with others, an almost pathological obsession with blindness, and a great concern for Oedipal involvement as important secondary themes. *El túnel* is a masterpiece depicting a case of pathological jealousy which effects the complete disintegration of a rational mind. It therefore stands as a classic example of the state of complete Existentialist isolation in which spatial and temporal considerations gradually disappear. The key to Castel's attempt to escape from his tunnel is the scene in his painting, "Maternidad," and it leads to María whom he seeks to possess physically and ultimately spiritually. And when neither type of possession is possible, Juan Pablo Castel realizes that he cannot—and never could—escape from the tunnel in which he has lived since childhood.

themes

In the relationship between Castel and María there are obvious Oedipal overtones. Jealousy and physical possession gradually assume important roles in the development of the action, and the tortured life of the protagonist is reflected on the level of the subconscious by a series of dreams, one of which has definite Kafkaesque interpretations. Reality, such as it is, is seen exclusively through the eyes of a disturbed painter. In no way does Sábato seek a return to nineteenth-century Realism, for the only Realism of *El túnel* is magical in nature, transporting the reader to the unreal world of the inconceivable from the very first line of the novel.

Sobre héroes y tumbas, the subject of the next three chapters, contains in a more developed manner the major themes of *El túnel* just as these same themes are observable in germinal form in the earlier volumes of essays. The means of presentation, however, are quite different. Whereas in the first novel the distorted world of Juan Pablo Castel is seen through the eyes of the protagonist, the second novel gives the reader a panoramic view of the whole of Argentina and especially of Buenos Aires from a great variety of vantage points. The present study will visit each of these vantage points in an attempt to define and describe the Argentina of Ernesto Sábato.

CHAPTER 4

Martín and Alejandra

SOBRE HÉROES Y TUMBAS, the subject of the next three chapters, stands as Sábato's most important work to date and as one of the truly great works of twentieth-century Argentine letters. Its long awaited publication in 1961, some thirteen years after the appearance of *El túnel*, was heralded in the press, and its subsequent acceptance by the reading public indicates that the novel was well worth the years of effort Sábato put into it. Writing for Sábato has never been a casual pastime engaged in for mere pleasure; it is a serious effort to analyze the great crises which confront man in his lifetime: the end of adolescence, the end of youth, the end of life itself. Limiting himself as he does to the crucial periods of existence, he has always preferred to restrict his literary production to those few works which he is willing to bring out into public view. Many of his manuscripts have been destroyed by their author, and still others have been reworked into *Sobre héroes y tumbas*. Writing in *El escritor y sus fantasmas*, Sábato states that he will be satisfied if before his death he is able to write one novel which will stand the test of time (*Escritor*, p. 16). *Sobre héroes y tumbas* may well be that novel.

The writing process has never been easy for Sábato. He reports that it is one of almost continuous suffering for him both from the spiritual as well as from the mental standpoint. In addition to a complete lack of confidence in the ultimate success of his work, Sábato experiences such physical afflictions as stomach ache, poor digestion, insomnia, and liver trouble. His writing schedule is highly irregular. Weeks and even months pass during which he writes nothing, allowing his thoughts to undergo a tortuous period of gestation. Then, when all of his ideas have taken form, he writes tumultuously. Later much of his manuscript is discarded, and that which remains is reworked, sometimes as many as five times.

Sobre héroes y tumbas stands as a classic example of Sábato's production technique. Running to over four hundred dense, compact pages in the original edition, it confronts the serious reader with many of the same physical and spiritual doubts that assail its creator. Sábato openly admits that he himself may not fully comprehend all of its symbolic and thematic ramifications, many of which have been subsequently offered by readers, critics, and even psychiatrists. But out of the pages certain lucid themes emerge from which valid conclusions indicative of Sábato's concept of twentieth-century Argentina may be drawn.

I   *The Obscure Labyrinth*

Ernesto Sábato's second novel is a national novel which seeks to present an analysis of contemporary Argentina from the historical, the demographic, and to a certain extent the geographic point of view. In contrast to *El túnel*, which was primarily the case study of an individual, *Sobre héroes y tumbas* is a vast, panoramic screen on which a series of provocative tableaux are alternately projected. Less than half a dozen primary characters appear in the first novel while a catalogue of the second reveals some twenty-five primary figures and dozens of secondary ones. The number of characters reaches almost astronomical novelistic proportions if one includes the hundreds of men who formed the army of Lavalle in the counterpoint scenes of nineteenth-century history which are intercalated in the first and fourth parts of the novel. The novelist's concept, therefore, is basically different in the two works. The second novel is conceptually closer to the essay, *El otro rostro del peronismo*, in which Sábato presented the historical influences which shaped the Argentina of 1955 and which resulted in the Perón dictatorship.

Although the novel is divided into four parts, there really are three basic plot divisions and one subdivision. In the present study these three divisions will be maintained, but it should be pointed out that all three ultimately fit together to form a unified theme which explores the obscure labyrinth leading to the primary secret of man's existence. Sábato struggled assiduously to give his drama a certain measure of unity to satisfy his readers' mania for finding order and relevance in events which perhaps have none. He offers his work as a testimony of some of the problems which have been experienced in recent years by the inhabitants of that extreme corner of the world that is Argentina.

The focus of most of the novel's action is on the city of Buenos Aires, and in many respects it may be considered *the* novel of the Argentine capital. There is, however, at the beginning and again at the end a kind of interplay between scenes which take place in the far north near the Bolivian border and in the south on the road to Patagonia which makes the novel national in its point of view. Historically the main threads of action take place in the twentieth century but in no precise order. The opening lines, for example, make reference to events which took place near the end of June, 1955, but the novel itself moves both forwards and backwards from this point in time. In the reminiscences of one of the characters the reader is transported back to the events of the British invasion of Buenos Aires of 1806-7, The Revolution of May in 1810, and the flight of Lavalle and his followers north to Bolivia in 1841 as a result of his disagreement with the dictator Rosas.

There is at the same time a conscious effort in *Sobre héroes y tumbas* to include representatives of the major national groups which today compose the Argentine population. Included are characters of Spanish origin and a rather large number of figures of Italian ancestry. These are the two dominant strains in the nation's ethnic composition. Likewise Sábato infuses into his novel characters of English, German, Jewish, Polish, and Indian backgrounds, thereby establishing a truly representative society of the Argentine citizenry. The various social strata which characterize the nation also appear in the book. Of the four protagonists, two are representatives of the decadent aristocracy of nineteenth-century Argentina and two are representatives of the category which might loosely be called middle class. These four characters are thrown into contact with a myriad of characters representing such elements as the aristocratic society of the Avenida Santa Fe, the world of industry and finance, the working class, and the humble society of those who live from hand to mouth. Despite their aristocratic and middle-class backgrounds,

several of the protagonists barely manage to escape falling
into the latter category and the vicissitudes of existence which
characterize it.

All of the characters of Sábato's second novel are fictitious
except for three or four figures lifted from the contemporary
scene. Most prominent of these figures are Jorge Luis Borges
and the Surrealist painter, Oscar Domínguez. References are
made to a number of other contemporary figures including
Perón, Anthony Eden, Ella Fitzgerald, and the late Carlos
Gardel who became a national idol with his interpretations
of the tango. None of these latter figures actually appears in
the novel, but Lavalle, the hero of the struggle against Rosas,
does appear in the historical scenes, and he even speaks to the
reader after his death in the northern province of Jujuy.

One can most successfully extricate the three basic plot
divisions of *Sobre héroes y tumbas* by considering them as stories
describing the crucial events in the lives of the four protagonists.
Although the threads of narrative woven about each character
may be analyzed separately, this in no way implies that their
lives were not intertwined. The exact opposite is true, although
to a degree each one experiences moments in the tunnel of
isolation which characterized the life of Juan Pablo Castel.
One of the characters, Fernando, does not even appear until the
third part of the novel, although his name is mentioned early
in the first part and his sinister relationship with another
protagonist, his daughter Alejandra, is suggested near the end
of part two. Fernando, nevertheless, may be considered the
dominant influence in the lives of the other three protagonists
and of all the other characters in the novel who come in contact
with his psychopathic personality.

The first plot division includes all of parts one and two of
the novel as well as a few pages of the fourth part. In this
study this plot division will be considered in the subsequent
subdivisions of the present chapter. It is the history of a tragic,
frustrating love affair between Martín del Castillo and
Alejandra Vidal Olmos, not unlike the affair between Juan
Pablo Castel and María Iribarne Hunter in *El túnel*. Martín,
however, is not Castel. An innocent, inexperienced youth of
seventeen, he first encounters Alejandra and falls in love with
her one Saturday in May, 1953. The confusing and perplexing

events of this romance are brought to an end on June 24, 1955 with the death of Alejandra and her father in a mysterious fire which swept their ancestral home in the Barracas district of Buenos Aires.

A variety of parallel actions occurs throughout this plot division, and all of the major themes of the novel are introduced in germinal form. Most important of these parallel actions is the history of the Olmos Acevedo family of which Alejandra and her father Fernando are the last descendants. The history of this ficticious family goes back to the colonial and independence periods, and about 1840 it is joined to the authentic account of the march of Lavalle northward to escape the forces of the dictator Rosas. This account is not concluded until the very end of the novel where sections dealing with the fate of Lavalle alternate with the final events in the story of Martín del Castillo.

Blindness is another theme which first occurred in *El túnel* in the case of Allende and which becomes a major subject of the second novel. Sábato confesses that the subject of blindness has always been an obsession with him, and the mere mention of the word by Martín shortly after meeting Alejandra is enough to bring about a violent reaction. Recollections of Alejandra's reaction to the word continue to puzzle Martín throughout their relationship, but it is not until much later in the novel that the motivation is clear.

The second plot division, considered here in the chapter called "An Idiot's Tale," is a nightmarish journey into the tortured mind of Fernando Vidal Olmos in which he offers the reader the results of his "scientific" investigations concerning the world of the blind. Rarely has the field of fiction offered such a fantastic, violent, schizophrenic view of the mind of a psychopath. Sábato has not gone without criticism for having shocked the sensibilities of certain elements of the reading public with this section, but he hastens to point out that many profound and honest individuals have risen in his defense. Furthermore, he affirms that no base or scandalous purpose motivated this "Informe sobre ciegos" ("A Study of the Blind"), and he suggests that those finding fault with the episode are victims of the dormant inclinations toward the lascivious which all men have.

To the charge that the "Informe sobre ciegos" is an incoherent digression in the novel, Sábato defends its inclusion as a means of representing the total character of Fernando Vidal Olmos. While it is true that the section of some one hundred pages could be omitted without seriously affecting the progress of the action, it nevertheless was included by its author for the purpose of defining symbolically the salient characteristics of his personality. Ostensibly it is the result of Fernando's "scientific" investigations into the subworld of the period from the time of his birth on June 24, 1911, to the middle of the twentieth century. It is interesting to note that the date of Fernando's birth coincides exactly with Sábato's and that the place of the former's birth, Capitán Olmos, is by Sábato's own admission a fictional representation of his native Rojas. An immediate conclusion is that certain elements of his own personality are to be found in all of the four major protagonists. There are, nevertheless, so many references to political activities similar to those engaged in by Sábato during his years in La Plata and Paris that a careful study of autobiographical elements in this section is indicated.

While much of this division contains episodes which verge on the fantastic, it is perhaps best to view it as a psychopath's concept of the world. There is no doubt that Fernando is mad, and his descent into the sewers of Buenos Aires which occupies a major portion of the section can be interpreted as a nightmarish view of the journey of life. Fernando is the key figure in the novel in the sense that he casts a sinister spell on all the other protagonists; his relationship with his own daughter Alejandra is incestuous; and it is his shadow which constantly intervenes to thwart the efforts of Martín and Alejandra to find love and understanding.

A fourth protagonist in *Sobre héroes y tumbas* is the pensive Bruno Bassán who appears in the first two parts as a friend of Alejandra and later of Martín. In the case of the latter he serves as confidant, and for Sábato he is a kind of interpreter and commentator on the action as it unfolds. Because of this role, many critics have seen Bruno as the author himself, forgetting at the same time that Fernando as well as Martín and Alejandra also are Sábato.

A consideration of Bruno leads to the third plot division and to the chapter titled "An Unknown God" in the present study. Although Bruno is an almost constant companion of Martín during the days of his affair with Alejandra, it is not until the last part of the novel that the previous references to his own life are tied together in a continuous narrative. The death of Alejandra and Fernando in the Barracas fire brings forth a flood of reminiscences in which Bruno recalls the days of his youth in Capitán Olmos and his association with Fernando and the Vidal Olmos family. These recollections to a degree are repetitious, but they serve the valuable purpose of analyzing the contradictory personality of Fernando from yet another point of view. Bruno also reveals a great deal about his own personality and about the conflict with Fernando into which he was inevitably drawn.

All of Bruno's commentaries serve to draw a kind of conclusion to the great number of chaotic events which have transpired in the course of the novel. The term "conclusion" is used here in the sense of a termination of activities, not as an interpretation of their ultimate meaning or of Sábato's intentions. Since Bruno is in every way a stable person, his narrative may be interpreted as another view of the same period of time covered in the fantastic episodes of the "Informe sobre ciegos." Beginning his story about 1911 in Capitán Olmos, he continues the narrative through the period of the fall of Yrigoyen in 1930. Communist and Anarchist movements similar to those mentioned by Fernando and experienced by Sábato himself conclude the section.

Bruno's tale leaves many unresolved problems just as the death of Alejandra in the mysterious fire in Barracas leaves Martín face to face with the enigma of existence. A visit to the ruins of the Vidal Olmos ancestral home renews the episodes of Lavalle's march toward the north in Martín's mind. The account which was begun in the first part of the novel now continues and alternates with the events in Martín's life following the fire. The interplay of nineteenth- and twentieth-century incidents continues to the end of the novel, the former serving as a counterpoint to the latter. Martín's desperation is resolved in one of the more tender scenes in the novel, and a kind of philosophy of hope is offered after more than four hundred pages of desperate frustration.

Sobre héroes y tumbas is, therefore, a kind of obscure labyrinth leading into the heart of the very soul of man. At the same time it seeks keys to explain the nature and purpose of existence. Sábato superimposes the national image on these problems to present a work that is both Argentine and universal at the same time. Whether he is successful in reaching the heart of the labyrinth remains to be decided at the conclusion of the present study.

II   *The Dragon and the Princess*

In no sense of the word does the relationship between Martín del Castillo and Alejandra Vidal Olmos follow any logical or meaningful chronological progression. While there is a beginning and an end, the period between these two extremes is one in which Martín and the reader are perplexed by a strange series of events which often seem to have no relationship to each other. Alejandra is seemingly oblivious to the enigmatic character of these incidents; at any rate she is totally unconcerned with the necessity of giving any order to things. The many uncertainties concerning her own life and activities are answered evasively, and at the end of the novel many of the conclusions regarding her personality are largely based on conjecture. One may conclude that Sábato never intended to provide complete answers to these problems if indeed there *are* answers to them.

A comparison of the opening lines of *El túnel* with those of the present novel under consideration shows a remarkable parallelism: a great deal of the action of each novel is revealed to the reader in the first paragraph. Castel begins his narrative with the revelation that he has killed María in a case so celebrated that every one of the readers must already know about it. Likewise the opening lines of *Sobre héroes y tumbas* describe the fire of June 24, 1955, and the subsequent death of Alejandra and Fernando. Mention is already made of their relationship during these disparate events.

The circumstances of the first meeting between Martín and Alejandra were so unusual that a kind of magical Realism similar to that established in the opening lines of *El túnel* grips the novel from its very beginning. Lounging on a park bench, Martín has the sensation that everything is different, that someone behind him is desperately attempting to communicate with him. Suddenly his eyes fall on the pale face of an unknown girl crossing the park. Although no words are exchanged, Martín knows that something crucial has happened in his life and that he will never be the same person again.

Many days later Martín is inevitably drawn to his accustomed spot in Lezama Park as if to keep a prearranged date. From a distance the same unknown girl rushes forward to meet him with the words, "I was waiting for you." Such telepathic communication is characteristic of Alejandra's personality, as Martín later discovers. Their subsequent meetings often occur by chance in the most unexpected places, while on other occasions their meetings are prearranged, usually in restaurants or *confiterías*. They frequently walk along the waterfront or exchange ideas in the remote corners of a park or plaza. "Things hardly ever happen," their mutual friend Bruno frequently states, and in their relationship few events do take place. Those incidents which do occur leave Martín so distraught that their value becomes highly dubious.

The long conversations between Martín, Alejandra, and a series of other characters who appear in the first two parts of the novel serve to introduce a great variety of themes, several of which are not terminated until near the end of the novel. Such a vast array of themes and figures has caused one critic to view *Sobre héroes y tumbas* as a work of Baroque art.[1] The dialogues may conveniently be separated into several planes. In the first place the central corpus of the Martín-Alejandra section is their frustrated affair pucntuated by long conversations in which they seek to communicate with each other and to establish a foundation for love. Other themes which appear in this same series include digressions into the childhood of the two protagonists and into the history of Alejandra's ancestors. On another plane are the conversations between Bruno and Martín by which a great deal of the novel is presented. Bruno serves as confessor to Martín and in many ways is a father figure to the distraught youth. Bruno also refers to his own life and to his association with Alejandra's family, but this does not become a major theme until the last part of the novel after the Barracas fire.

Throughout this section Martín comes in contact with a number of figures representing a variety of middle- and lower-class types of Buenos Aires life. At times he is only a distracted listener to the details of their sometimes serious, sometimes trifling conversation. On one occasion Martín's thoughts and the conversation of several of his friends occur in parallel columns on the printed page. One of the more perplexing conversations of the novel takes place between Martín and a friend of Alejandra who owns a publishing house. Martín's purpose is to seek work as a proofreader, and he is unable to comprehend why such an important person as Alejandra's friend would take so much time to talk with him, especially when it becomes evident that no work is available. Near the end of this section (during the period of the burning of the churches in Buenos Aires before the downfall of Perón), Martín, caught up in the violent street fighting, comes to the assistance of a wealthy lady trying to save valuable works of religious art from the churches. Their conversation is one of the few commentaries on the Perón dictatorship which controlled Argentina during most of the time of the action of the novel.

Critics have generally agreed that Sábato's feminine characters are presented more convincingly than are his masculine ones. This is certainly true in the case of Martín and Alejandra, although the generalization does not seem valid in the case of Fernando and Juan Pablo Castel. Throughout *Sobre héroes y tumbas* Martín constantly appears in the role of an almost innocent victim of the circumstances in which he exists. Only rarely does he actively attempt to alter the course of the flow of events into which he is swept. Introspective and analytical by nature, he is more content asking Bruno to interpret these happenings to him. A key to his personality is the fact that from the very moment of his conception he was rejected by his mother who complained bitterly that he was the result of her carelessness. Alejandra, a person not easily surprised, is nevertheless unprepared for Martín's statement that his mother was a sewer, a *madrecloaca*. Knowing that she attempted unsuccessfully to abort during the period she was carrying him,

Martín develops a hatred for his mother that quite possibly explains the almost childlike role he plays opposite the more mature and more experienced Alejandra.

Although Martín's relationship with his father is of a less violent nature, it could hardly be called communicative. The two of them lived for years under the same roof, but their lives were as separate as if they had been living on two different islands, separated by a vast abyss. The fact that Martín's father was an unsuccessful painter caused the son to view him with a sense of shame which ultimately turned into suppressed hatred. Again it is possible to consider Bruno a father figure who replaces the rejected natural father.

Surrounded as he is by feelings of remorse, rejection, and isolation, Martín seems bent on an effort to escape from the dregs of his existence and to seek a refuge in purity. Sábato offers five key words which explain Martín's existence: cold, cleanliness, snow, solitude, Patagonia. If one were to view the events in Martín's life related in this novel as the crisis of the end of youth, it would be possible to relate these key words to the incidents described. The frigid relationship with both parents is the initial cause of despair; as his life becomes less attractive he seeks an escape and a means of cleansing his soul. Love and finally sex seem to offer this snowy blanket of purity, but as Sábato indicated earlier in the essay *Heterodoxia* and in *El túnel*, sex only leads to a state of more extreme anguish and solitude. Patagonia is a geographical representation of the first four key words in Martín's life. In the novel it serves as a haven for Martín at the height of his desperation. Although Sábato has disagreed with many of the symbolic interpretations of various aspects of the novel, this austral region, rich in mineral and stock-raising potential, may easily be considered as a haven for the nation in its present economic plight. The many references to Patagonia in the novel and the alternate mention of the north in the Lavalle episodes give a geographic unity to the novel which would otherwise be lacking because of the concentration of action in the city of Buenos Aires.

In the first part of the novel Alejandra's family history is a kind of mystery, although this is not due to a dearth of details. It is due more to the fact that so many disconnected details are presented, causing confusion, and at the end of the novel certain aspects of Alejandra's relationship with her father are still somewhat vague. Her role in the novel has occasioned many a polemic, but a careful analysis of the text and of Sábato's subsequent statements in *El escritor y sus fantasmas* greatly clarifies her position. Physically she is a combination of European stock with the characteristics of high cheekbones and Mongoloid eyes found in the Indian. A mixture of contradictory feelings and sentiments which such a diversified racial background would suggest are evident in her serious eyes and somewhat disdainful mouth. Sábato's purpose was to describe a typically Argentine woman, but the interpretation that Alejandra represents the entire nation has been advanced by numerous critics much to the author's surprise. The fact, however, that her name contains the same number of letters as the word Argentina and that it also begins and ends with the same letter is perhaps more than coincidental.

Throughout the first half of the novel Alejandra is the dominant figure, although it later becomes apparent that she herself was dominated most of her life by the sinister effect of Fernando. Martín by comparison is meek and submissive to her many whims and inexplicable fluctuations. Bruno once felt a kind of infatuation for her, but there is no indication that she responded to him in any way. Her mysterious appearances and disappearances throughout the entire period of her affair with Martín are accepted by him, if reluctantly. Only near the end, when it is apparent that he is destined to lose her completely, does he make a futile effort to keep her.

Most of the salient characteristics of Alejandra's personality first became evident during Martín's first visit to her home in the Barracas district in the southern part of the capital. It is interesting to note that Sábato chose a specific home in Barracas as a model for the ancestral home of the Olmos Acevedo family. After a long search he elected what he felt was a suitable house in which to place his fictional characters. The home described in the novel contained a large bay window which commanded a view of the entire district. Since the model house did not contain such a bay window, another one on Yrigoyen Street was also studied, and a composite of the two buildings was used in the novel.

As Martín first approaches the house with Alejandra, he is confronted by a structure which reveals a glorious past but which now stands in a state of disrepair in the midst of a district filled with factories and humble dwellings. Darkness shrouds the entire scene except for one illuminated room; the silence is broken only by random notes from a clarinet. Here Sábato introduces two of the novel's major themes. As Martín follows Alejandra up the dark circular stairway, he casually remarks that such a place is fine for the blind. Her reaction, described earlier in the present chapter, is not fully comprehended by Martín or by the reader until after the discovery of the "Informe sobre ciegos" which survived the fire. The clarinet notes come from the distant room of Bebe, the brother of Alejandra's mother, who is one of the surviving members of the Olmos Acevedo family whose history goes back to the colonial period.

During the same night Alejandra experiences a fit which closely resembles epilepsy. Similar fits occur throughout the period of their affair, but their exact nature is never revealed. Martín is also introduced to additional unexpected sides to Alejandra's personality on the same memorable night. Interspersed throughout the first part are flashbacks which serve to illumine certain incidents in Alejandra's past. Some of these incidents are told in the third person, in which case italics are used. Still others are narrated by Alejandra herself both before and after the epileptic fit. On one occasion at the age of eleven she left home principally to get the attention of her grandparents and other relatives. Seeking refuge in an abandoned house, she started a fire to keep warm until such time when she was returned home by the police. Whether this relatively minor incident has a direct relationship to the fire which later destroyed Alejandra and Fernando is a matter of conjecture. As a result of this adventure and the subsequent punishment, Alejandra entered into a kind of religious fervor which lasted until she was fifteen. Certain of her religious trances greatly resemble the fits which she later experiences. The recollection of these religious experiences, in fact, brings on the first seizure which Martín witnesses.

Another curious incident from Alejandra's youth is her experiences with Marcos Molina, an acquaintance whom she met during her visits to the beach at vacation time. Two similar incidents separated by a year serve to throw light on Alejandra's early attitudes regarding sex. In both cases Alejandra bathes in the nude with Marcos. Both times he resists her plan, but each time he is shamed by her until he finally agrees. The first incident ostensibly is used by Alejandra to prove that sex is a ridiculous act and that one can just as easily resist its temptations in the nude as fully clothed. When the incident occurs again a year later, the conservative Catholic Marcos is scandalized and suggests that their immodest actions will bring down the wrath of God. To this idea Alejandra screams that God does not exist and laughs openly at such ideas as hell and eternal punishment. This second incident when Alejandra was seventeen marks a definite end to her period of religious rapture and confirms her complete rejection of religious, spiritual, and moral values in the Christian sense.

Three impressions regarding Alejandra emerge from the activities experienced by Martín during his first visit to the home. The first of these impressions is that he will never completely know or understand Alejandra. Although they were physically close—and eventually this was to become physical intimacy—spiritually they were separated by a profound abyss. As in the case of Juan Pablo Castel and María Iribarne Hunter, sexual intimacy only served to widen their spiritual separation. But enigmatic as their relationship was, a second impression stood out clearly: Alejandra needed and even had elected him. Somehow she had chosen him from among the teeming millions of Buenos Aires and had confessed things to him which she had never before confessed to anybody. Martín suspected that there were untold thousands of ideas still within her and that many of them would never be revealed to him. One of these untold secrets concerned the name Fernando, which Alejandra had almost involuntarily mentioned only to refuse to clarify who he was when pressed by Martín. The third impression received by Martín concerned Alejandra's strange behavior when he casually mentioned the blind. It is later apparent that Fernando and blindness are part of the same impression, but such a relationship could not yet be evident to Martín on the basis of the fragmentary knowledge available to him.

All of these impressions are summarized in one brief paragraph which serves to point out in addition the relationship of Martín to Alejandra and to the universe: "Night, infancy, shadows, shadows, the terror of blood, blood, flesh and blood, dreams, abysses, unfathomable abysses, solitude solitude solitude, we touch but we remain incommensurable distances apart, we touch but we are alone. He was a child under an immense dome, in the middle of the dome, in the midst of terrifying silence, alone in that gigantic universe" (*Héroes*, p. 65). This quotation has a direct relationship to three dreams which are described in the first part of the novel. The first dream occurrs moments before one of the early meetings of Martín and Alejandra as he dozes on a bench in Lezama Park. In the course of the dream Martín is being transported aimlessly in an abandoned boat along a wide river. Through the shadows he can see an impenetrable jungle rise on the shore as if it were a wall shrouding a secret, dangerous way of life behind it. A muffled voice seems to call him from the solitude of the jungle. As he desperately seeks to raise himself to hear the voice more clearly, he awakes to find Alejandra beside him. The symbolism of the dream is readily apparent: the jungle represents their future life together, and its mysterious, esoteric characteristics only serve to accentuate the immense solitude of Martín and Alejandra as previously seen in the quotation cited.

Alejandra later relates a dream to Martín in which she desperately tries to see and hear a priest speaking from the pulpit of a cathedral. As she nears the pulpit, she sees to her horror that he has no face or hair, and his words are drowned out by the furious clanging of the cathedral bells which she discovers to be the bells of Santa Lucía, the church she attended as a child. Again relating this dream to the events summarized in the above quotation, one sees Alejandra's struggle from childhood to comprehend the symbolism of Christian theology only to discover that the priest is faceless—at least his face is invisible to her—and his words are unintelligible mutterings over the cacophony of the bells. Salvation, if it exists, is unattainable for Alejandra as she wanders through the shadows of solitude. At the same time, Alejandra describes to Martín the recurrence of fire in her dreams and asks him if he does not find something sacred and enigmatic about fire. Knowing as the reader does that Alejandra is ultimately to be consumed by flames, he is better prepared to answer her question than

is Martín. The invisible face of the priest will be used at a later
point to introduce the title of the second part of the novel as
will Martín's second dream which has a similar central symbol.

Although Martín and Alejandra dominate the action of the
first part of the novel, a large number of other characters is
introduced which present a representative group of figures from
all levels of Buenos Aires society. Most of these characters are
either acquaintances of Martín or of Bruno, and their comments
on current events and problems introduce divergent views
of the national problem. Secondary characters continue to
appear throughout the rest of the novel, so that at its conclusion one feels that he has met at least one representative of
every major segment of the Argentine population. In a similar
fashion, Sábato successfully injects a variety of viewpoints
concerning major political and social issues of contemporary
Argentina. While almost all of these ideas come from the mouths
of fictional characters, at least on one occasion figures from
contemporary history are asked to step forth from the pages
of the novel to offer their viewpoint and to allow fictional
characters to analyze it.

Among this vast array of secondary figures is Chichín,
the owner of a pizza house where many of Martín's acquaintances gather to pass the time discussing a variety of issues.
While Chichín serves the author's purpose as the owner of
a central gathering place for a number of these minor characters,
he himself is not a carefully drawn figure as are certain others
of the group. Bucich and Humberto J. D'Arcángelo are without
a doubt the most important of these secondary characters.
The former is a truck driver for the Transporte Patagónico, a
veritable man of the open road who has spent his life trucking
produce between Buenos Aires and Patagonia. With his
positive, somewhat optimistic philosophy of life he stands
as a distinct contrast to the disillusioned majority. Described
as a somewhat stooped giant with grey hair and a childlike
expression, Bucich represents a way of escape for Martín from
the frustrations of the metropolis, and in the final scene of
the novel Martín is on his way south in one of the Transporte
Patagónico trucks. Bucich at times assumes the role of a
father figure in much the same way that Bruno does. Bruno,
however, is a contemplative sort of person while Bucich's
view of life is closely related to direct action.

Humberto J. D'Arcángelo, the son of an Italian immigrant, represents a sizable segment of the population of Buenos Aires where nearly a third of the inhabitants are of Italian ancestry. Always carrying a folded copy of the newspaper *Crítica*, Tito, as the younger D'Arcángelo is called, is a kind of self-appointed sports analyst and political commentator. The typical Argentine passion for football is incarnate in Tito, a fan of the popular Boca Juniors team. His knowledge of the sport and of its past and present heroes is almost encyclopedic, and his disillusionment with the mediocre quality of the sport today is no less than his disillusionment as he views the contemporary political scene. Bribery and theft are the only governmental policies Tito has seen, and his life has covered periods of Conservative, Radical, and Peronist rule. Likewise he has lost faith in the military as an effective instrument for political reform. The true heroes of history—Edison, the inventor of the telegraph, the old "German" with the long mustache who cures African natives—have all, in Tito's opinion, died penniless and forgotten. This is proof of his theory that the sacrifices of others only serve to enrich the opportunist.

Sábato states in the novel itself that these scenes in Chichín's pizzeria are an attempt to describe the tendencies toward bitterness, unbelief, irony, resentment, and candor which typify a certain kind of Argentine. At the same time a certain element of hope persists through the thick haze of bitter disillusionment. It is this element of hope which Sábato mentions at various times in the novel that ultimately offers Martín a *modus vivendi* if not a solution to the complex labyrinth of existence.

Characteristic of the social level which Chichín, Bucich, and Tito represent is their manner of speaking which Sábato faithfully reproduces. The structure, pronunciation, and vocabulary of their dialogue is essentially that of the unrefined speech of La Boca, the port district of Buenos Aires famous as the cradle of the tango and as the home of the Boca Juniors football club. A great deal of the action of *Sobre héroes y tumbas* takes place in La Boca and in the contingent district of Barracas where Alejandra's home is located. Typical of the speech of this area is the use of a great number of Italian words as well as idioms and slang expressions which are at times almost unintelligible to the reader inexperienced in the highly regional speech patterns of the area.

In sum, the pizzeria scenes represent an effort on the part of the author to paint a canvas filled with superimposed glimpses of life in the lower income districts of Buenos Aires. These scenes are, in the opinion of Sábato, much more typical of life in Argentina than are the stereotyped views of gaucho life and folklore with which the casual tourist is regaled. Both hope and despair—the latter in generous quantity—are evident in the everyday life of the typical resident of the area. A view of home life is provided when Tito invites the destitute Martín to his home so that he can at least have a meal and a temporary place to sleep. Tito's father still lives in the past and is, in the words of his son, a victim of progress, since the automobile has replaced the carriages he once drove. Their home is a combination of a dilapidated apartment and a stable where the odor of manure prevails. Tito's treasures are some faded photographs of football heroes, one of them personally dedicated to him, an ancient phonograph, and some tango records. The elder D'Arcángelo is a widower of three years, and Tito's seven brothers and sisters either have died or have left home for a different if not a better life. Tito himself offers a summary of his life and of that of his neighbors when he repeats the lines of a tango which lament the fact that everything good in life has gone never to return.

It is the complex personality of Alejandra which gives the title, "El dragón y la princesa," to the first part of the novel. As the story of her affair with Martín unfolds and as details of her past are revealed, the many sides to her personality fall together into one vast, distorted picture. The juxtaposition of one facet upon another creates an image of desperation as Alejandra seeks release from her prison and from the dark inner forces which hold her. At times she is contradictory, moving from a mood of unrestrained joy to deep melancholy without a moment's notice. It is all as if Martín were a prince who returns to find his princess sleeping in a grotto guarded by a vicious dragon. But the exasperating aspect of Alejandra's case is that the dragon is not visible; it is totally within her. Alejandra is a kind of monstrous dragon-princess in which a constant interior struggle takes place. When these struggles become violent, they result in open warfare evident in the epileptic fits which Alejandra suffers or in violent nightmares which shake her sleeping body.

The mystery of Alejandra is inexplicably linked in Martín's mind to his feeling for his mother. Owing to the deep-seeded feeling of rejection which he experienced from the days of his early childhood, he finds it difficult to enter into a normal relationship with Alejandra. Most difficult of all are the physical aspects of love, for he has come to associate the sexual act with his own unwanted birth. His great sentimental attachment to Alejandra serves to help him overcome these feelings, yet the moment physical relations are suggested Alejandra becomes disturbed by the rumblings of the dragon within her.

Martín could not help but remember the two incidents which Alejandra described in which she and Marcos Molina swam in the nude. On the second occasion the more mature Alejandra attempted to seduce Marcos, and consequently Martín could not interpret her hesitancy with him as anything but a rejection of his love for her. Again the reader is reminded of the maternal rejection suffered by Martín, and this same feeling with Alejandra is almost identical to the rejection felt by Juan Pablo Castel in his affair with María who obviously is a mother symbol. In the case of Martín and Alejandra the identity of the dragon within the latter is not clear at the end of the first part of the novel, and at the end of the second part it is only suggested with the appearance of Fernando for the first time. At the time of the death of the father and the daughter in the Barracas fire the nature of their sinister relationship has only been revealed symbolically, but the careful reader is able to identify the dragon which so tormented Alejandra's life and the lives of all who had the misfortune to encounter it.

On one occasion after an especially violent nightmare, Alejandra arises and takes a prolonged bath. She explains her long delay to Martín by stating that she was covered with filth and consequently needed an abnormal amount of time to cleanse herself. The naïveté of her ideas amuses her, but it nevertheless is another indication of a basic motif of the novel which Sábato always manages to keep just beneath the surface of the action. It is the desire of various characters, and especially of Martín and Alejandra, to free themselves from the chains of their sordid surroundings and to find a pure existence. Such basic desires may also be extended to include the Argentine population as a whole in a period when the nation is only a vague promise of its potential greatness. The desperation of Martín and Alejandra is typical of the entire country, although it should be indicated that its cause in their case is essentially psychological. Disillusionment with the political scene is more evident in the case of Humberto J. D'Arcángelo and his friends, and although Martín is often present when they discuss these national issues, his thoughts usually are on the enigmatic actions of Alejandra.

The events in the first months of their love affair, although frequently distressing and unpleasant, are among the happiest moments in Martín's life. As he later relates them to Bruno, the two of them attempt to discover a key to the entire relationship and to give order and logic to incidents which, in Sábato's own words, perhaps have none. At this point in the narrative the motivation behind Alejandra's strange reaction to the mention of blindness and the identity of Fernando are still puzzles whose solution must come later.

III   *Lavalle and Other Heroes*

While most of the action of *Sobre héroes y tumbas* takes place in a two-year period before the 1955 fire which destroyed the Olmos Acevedo home, there is a series of historical flashbacks which form a superstratum over which the contemporary action takes place. In *El otro rostro del peronismo* Sábato speaks of a common infancy of all Argentines, a set of shared traditions and values passed on from generation to generation. The present is therefore a composite of past events, and the actors who shaped these events are the spiritual parents of the present generation. Life is a play acted out on a stage built over the heroes and tombs of the past.

Such a continuity of history does not necessarily imply that the past always remains submerged in its tomb. Quite the contrary is true; Sábato believes that events of remote history are often mysteriously linked to the present. Occasionally they rise to the surface stimulated by some absurd but powerful force such as a song, a joke, or an old antagonism. As in the case of the essay, *El otro rostro del peronismo*, the twentieth-century tragedy of Argentina is a result of decades of injustice to the forgotten masses—first the gaucho, then the immigrants, and finally the laboring class. Perón was not an isolated phenomenon in the course of Argentine history but rather the answer, if a demagogic one, to an unfulfilled cry for justice. According to Sábato there is in every Argentine citizen an element of Perón; he is a part of the common history shared by the entire nation.

The same idea of a common shared history is evident in the four protagonists of Sábato's latest novel. History may be viewed vertically in the case of Alejandra and Fernando and horizontally in the case of Martín and Bruno. These viewpoints refer to the historical depth given to the family of Alejandra and Fernando while in the case of Martín and Bruno only details concerning their immediate families are offered. Through his relationship with Alejandra, Martín is caught up in the complex web of the Olmos Acevedo family, and on the occasion of his first visit to her home in Barracas the confused tale of the family begins when Alejandra shows him an old lithograph tacked on the wall of her room. The lithograph shows a group of tattered army regulars, the remains of the glorious Legion of Lavalle gathered around the body of the fallen leader.

Juan Lavalle is an almost legendary figure of the struggle against the dictator Rosas. Born in Buenos Aires in 1797, he entered armed service at the age of fifteen and rose rapidly in rank as a result of distinguished service in the siege of Montevideo and in the campaigns against the Spanish forces in Chile and Peru. By 1826 he had become a general of the army. His most controversial act was his struggle against Dorrego, the great defender of Federalism who became governor of the province of Buenos Aires in 1827 after the resignation of Rivadavia, the nation's first president. Dorrego as governor of the most important province became the *de facto* president of the infant nation, but his political beliefs were anathema to the Unitarians and their followers. He was instrumental in concluding a peace treaty with Brazil, but the veterans of this campaign were highly dissatisfied with the terms of the

treaty. Lavalle, upon his return, declared himself governor
of Buenos Aires and led his troops into the heart of the city.
Dorrego fled but was pursued by Lavalle who found him in
the hands of his soldiers and shot him within the hour.

The assassination of Dorrego precipitated the bloody conflict of the Rosas era which did not terminate until the
dictator's final defeat in the Battle of Monte Caseros in 1852.
Lavalle became one of the most active opposers of Rosas
during the decade beginning about 1830 when his troops began
a series of campaigns which took them from the province of
Buenos Aires through most of the major provinces of the north.
Gradually, as the result of numerous defeats in 1840 and 1841,
he was forced to flee northward toward the Bolivian border.
On October 8, 1841, while the general was resting in a house
in Jujuy, a Federalist patrol surprised the remnants of his
once formidable army and shot the hero of the resistance
against Rosas. Undaunted, his forces gathered around his
body, swearing never to allow it to fall into the hands of the
Federalists who had declared their intention to decapitate the
remains and display Lavalle's head throughout the country.
Although they were unable to realize their ambition, it was
not for want of effort on their part. The heroic flight of
Lavalle's followers toward Bolivia was interrupted only
briefly to remove the bones from the decomposing body.
They were transported across the border to safety while the
remains of his flesh were washed back into the rivers of
Argentina where they could return to their homeland.

The history of Lavalle is intercalated throughout the first
and fourth parts of *Sobre héroes y tumbas*. Various narrators
relate the thread of the action: Alejandra, her great-grandfather Pancho, Sábato himself, various members of Lavalle's
legion, and even Lavalle. Two figures in the history, Colonel
Bonifacio Acevedo and an ensign, Celedonio Olmos, are
the great-uncle and the father of Pancho Olmos, respectively.
Here the reader is transported back into history to the colonial
period as he is alternately introduced first to members of the
Acevedo family and then to the Olmos.

At this point Alejandra's great-grandfather Pancho continues
the family history, explaining the respective roles of the Olmos
and Acevedo branches of the family in the Legion of Lavalle.

Celedonio Olmos and Bonifacio Acevedo are the two family members who accompanied Lavalle on his flight toward Bolivia. In a series of alternate scenes, some related by Pancho and others spoken by the very participants in the march, the whole history of Lavalle from the days of the Chilean and Peruvian campaigns to the assassination of Dorrego and the ill-fated resistance to Rosas unfolds. When the Lavalle episode temporarily terminates near the end of the first part of the novel, the remnants of his forces are faced with the task of saving his putrefying remains from the hands of the pursuing Federalists.

Sábato does not continue the tale of Lavalle until near the end of the fourth part of the novel, and there he takes it up at a point prior to the final events related in the first part. Lavalle is still alive, leading his troops through the province of Salta. The decimation of the Unitarian forces throughout the nation is nearly complete, and their only hope is in the popular General Paz who still is strong enough to resist.

Many critics have offered a variety of opinions as to why Sábato inserted the Lavalle episode in *Sobre héroes y tumbas.* Clearly it was not necessary, since the distant relationship of Alejandra to two of Lavalle's followers is a fact which contributes very little to the narrative. On the other hand, the Lavalle episode forms a kind of counterpoint to the contemporary action. It gives the novel a panoramic perspective and, in the words of Sábato, a feeling of the contradiction and synthesis between the historical and the atemporal found in every man. He further affirms that his purpose was to show that in the time of Lavalle the same as today, man was faced by the eternal problems of birth, hope, disillusion, and finally death. At a later point in the present study this episode will be related to the basic philosophy of hope which the novelist offers in the case of Martín del Castillo.

Another aspect of the Lavalle episode which should not be overlooked is the great contrast which these nineteenth-century heroes offer when compared to the present determiners of Argentine history. "But at least in those days they knew why they were fighting: they desired liberty for the whole continent, they struggled for a great Nation. But today. . ." (*Héroes*, p. 339). There can be no doubt that Sábato was seeking a period of true heroism to offer as an example of what Argentina desperately needs today to save itself from chaos. The essay, *El otro rostro del peronismo*, clearly states that this same spirit for good still exists in the hearts of his countrymen, but his spirit can just as easily be appropriated by a demagogue as the recent history of Argentina so clearly demonstrates.

The Lavalle episode has resulted in the production of a popular record which first appeared in May, 1965, under the title *Romance de la Muerte de Lavalle*.[2] Although there have been suggestions that this same episode might lend itself to a film, the record is the first attempt to translate a portion of *Sobre héroes y tumbas* to another artistic medium. Sábato himself reads selections from his novel while the guitar and the voice of the popular Eduardo Falú offer a musical backdrop along with the chorus of Francisco Javier Ocampo and a traditional *vidalita* sung by Mercedes Sosa. The result is a most effective interpretation of probably the most poetic and moving portions of the novel, and its great popular success is due to inspire other efforts to adapt portions of the novel.

IV *Invisible Faces*

In the second part of the novel Sábato offers the reader a composite picture of Buenos Aires and of the multitude which populates this megalopolis at the month of the Río de la Plata. Additional evidence of Alejandra's unusual personality is presented, and the stage is set for a tentative solution to some of the vast array of problems which the novel investigates. The final scene of this section describes the bombing of the Plaza de Mayo and the burning of the churches of Buenos Aires during the last hectic weeks before the downfall of Perón in 1955.

In the first part of the novel there are only occasional references to national problems; most commonly these issues are raised as complaints made by Humberto J. D'Arcángelo as he philosophizes in Chichín's pizzeria. But in the second part a very real problem is presented: What is Argentina? The problem could best be viewed in an alternate form: Who is Argentina? Bruno, in this case a spokesman for Sábato, answers his own question with a series of disconnected thoughts: "nothing and everything . . . six million souls . . . six million

Argentines, Spaniards, Italians, Basques, Germans, Hungarians, Russians, Poles, Yugoslavs, Czechs, Syrians, Lebanese, Lithuanians, Greeks, Ukrainians . . . oh, Babylon . . . nothing and everything" (*Héroes*, pp. 138-40). Such random thoughts do in a sense identify the strange admixture that is Argentina. Bruno reaches only one conclusion, and it is directly related to the idea of isolation so skillfully presented in *El túnel*. He imagines that lost in this multitude of Buenos Aires is a single Tartar, unknown, immortal, and insignificant. In Bruno's mind this single Tartar is worth all the other millions of souls together, because no solitary being may be left alone in his solitude. The plea of Bruno (and of Sábato) is for the basic dignity and worth of the individual even when that individual is lost in the whirlpool of metropolitan life. Bruno's isolated Tartar is no different from the solitary Juan Pablo Castel who wanders over the streets of Buenos Aires seeking one person with whom he may communicate.

Throughout the second part of the novel Sábato more overtly introduces political issues of the mid-1950's in an attempt to show the violent divisive forces at work in the country. Such divisions, of course, go back historically to the nineteenth century, although the actors in the struggle are aware only of present frustrations. Bruno again is the source of these comments as he meditates perpetually on the meaning of existence in general and on the reality of that obscure region of the world in which he and his compatriots live and suffer. Sábato later indicates that it is an investigation of these same problems which inspires him to write and which to a degree makes an otherwise cheerless life bearable. If there indeed are solutions to these problems, Sábato never offers them to the reader. Rather, he is content at the end of the novel to present a *modus vivendi* which permits him as well as Martín del Castillo to continue their eternal struggle.

Two dreams near the end of the first part of the novel serve to introduce the idea of invisible faces, the major theme of the second part. The first of these two dreams is the one previously discussed in which Alejandra desperately seeks to hear the words of a priest in a cathedral only to discover that he has no face at all. A few pages later Martín has a similar dream: a beggar approaches him from the midst of a multitude

and opens a small bundle, revealing its contents to him. Martín
is unable to see the beggar's face, and as he departs, he mumbles
unintelligible words. The dream in itself was not repulsive or
disagreeable, but the anguish of its elusive meaning left
Martín in a state of desperation as if he had received an
important letter whose words were indecipherable, disfigured,
and obliterated by time.

In both dreams the face of the principal figure is invisible,
and the words which are spoken are incomprehensible to
Alejandra in the case of the first dream and to Martín in the
case of the second. An interesting point is the fact that
Alejandra, who frequently describes herself as covered with
filth, dreams that she is in a cathedral where she might expect
words of salvation for her tarnished soul. Martín, on the other
hand, is presented as an innocent, inexperienced youth, yet
in his dream a beggar approaches him with a filthy bundle
of nondescript articles. But the invisible faces of the priest
and the beggar are only two of the many such faces which
appear throughout the second part of *Sobre héroes y tumbas*.
Although in terms of their external features these other
faces are "visible," the enigmatic motivations behind their
actions are no more clear than are the words of the priest and
the beggar. At the same time, these people *are* Argentina, the
invisible Argentina, to borrow a term from Eduardo Mallea's
Historia de una pasión argentina.

Through Alejandra and Bruno, Martín is successively
introduced to first one and then another of these people who
make up the population of Buenos Aires. One of the most
puzzling of these encounters is the one with Alejandra's
friend Molinari, owner of a printing company where Martín
goes in search of employment. For some unexplained reason
Molinari takes Martín into his sumptuous office and devotes
more than an hour of his time telling him why he is unable
to give him employment and how he is sure that Martín would
not expect him to give him work just because Alejandra is a
mutual friend. Martín is so confused by the long interview
which Molinari grants to a nonentity that he leaves the
building nauseated and uncertain as to the kind of friendship
which binds Alejandra and Molinari.

No less clear is Alejandra's relationship to Bordenave, an unscrupulous adventurer who moves about Buenos Aires in an elegant sports car. Martín first meets Bordenave when Alejandra is in the process of arranging the interview with Molinari. Disturbingly he reappears at unexpected moments, often in the company of Alejandra who never attempts to explain their relationship. Martín begins to go through a series of questions and painful analyses in an attempt to explain this mysterious liaison. This painful process is not at all unlike the questioning engaged in by Juan Pablo Castel as he attempts to discover the relationship between María and Hunter and between María and her husband Allende. While Castel eventually reaches the unhappy truth behind María's actions, Martín never does discover the rather obvious fact that Alejandra is the mistress of Molinari, of Bordenave, and probably of several other men.

Strangely enough it is not until the second part of the novel that Martín meets Bruno for the first time. Alejandra arranges this meeting in a downtown café where Bruno is conversing with Méndez, a Communist friend. The reader is momentarily puzzled by this meeting, since Bruno and Martín have been seen together from the very first page of the novel. The explanation is that the events of the first part, while they occurred prior to the first meeting of Bruno and Martín, were later retold in detail by the latter in a long series of conversations which quite possibly took place even after Alejandra's death. The point of all this is that chronology of action is completely absent form *Sobre héroes y tumbas* as it often is in the contemporary novel. Sábato himself indicated in the introduction to the novel that events often lack order and relationship, and here as in the earlier *El túnel* he attempts to focus the reader's attention on the events themselves, not on their chronology or on their interrelationship.

A group of faces from another segment of Buenos Aires society comes into view as a result of Alejandra's decision to take employment in a *boutique* owned and operated by Wanda, a frivolous dressmaker who caters to women of high society. The fact that Alejandra would voluntarily associate herself with such elements is not in keeping with her personality and actions up to this point in the novel. Martín pays her a visit in this new world and is unable to define in his own mind her role in this new environment. It is as if she is wearing a mask, a thought which recalls to his mind the theory of Bruno that everyone has a series of masks which he uses according to the situation at hand. Martín's greatest problem is to ascertain which is Alejandra's true mask, for indeed the person he sees in Wanda's *boutique* is not the same Alejandra he met in Lezama Park.

One of the more comical yet pathetic types introduced in the first *boutique* scene is the effeminate, affected Quique. Ostensibly a newspaper theater critic, Quique delights Wanda and her friends with his inimitable tales of actors and actresses, which he punctuates with indelicate expressions and numerous French and English phrases. In a subsequent visit to the *boutique* Martín is again reminded of Bruno's theory of the masks when he happens to see Quique alone in a meditative mood. Quique is unaware of Martín's presence, and as Martín observes the pathetic figure, the words of Bruno flow through his mind:

> We always . . . wear a mask, a mask that never is the same but which changes for each one of the roles assigned to us in life: that of the professor, the lover, the intellectual, the deceived husband, the hero, the loving brother. But which mask do we wear, which one do we use when we are alone, when we think that no one is observing us, is controlling us, is listening to us, is needing us, is begging us, is confiding in us, is attacking us? Perhaps the sacred nature of such an instant is due to the fact that man is at such a time face to face with Divinity, or at least face to face with his own conscience. And perhaps we fail to pardon a person caught in this ultimate stage of nudity, the most terrible and most basic form of nudity, for it reveals the soul without any means of defense. (*Héroes*, p. 191)

As Martín approaches a second time, he exaggerates his footsteps to warn Quique of his presence and to allow him to assume one of his masks. Immediately he begins to chatter about Alejandra's family and about the importance of surnames as determiners of one's place in society. For four pages he engages in what amounts to a monologue, and Martín all the while experiences the agony of frustration since he has come to Wanda's not to listen to Quique's ramblings but to make a last effort to win back Alejandra.

There no doubt is a relationship between the segment of society represented by Wanda, Quique, and their associates and the shallow, frivolous world represented by Hunter and his frivolous cousin Mimí in *El túnel*. Both Quique and Mimí are ridiculous figures who enjoy using the same French expressions in their conversation. In both novels the patter of idle conversation comes at a point of deep anguish. Castel has come to Hunter's ranch in an attempt to pierce the curtain of mystery surrounding María; Martín has come to the *boutique* on a similar mission. The ensuing conversations only serve to delay and frustrate Castel and Martín, but at the same time Sábato succeeds in painting a picture of the hollowness of the society which Mimí and Quique represent. Although the delay which these interludes cause is frustrating to the respective protagonists, it should be pointed out that their subsequent attempts to communicate with their lovers after this obstacle has been removed are fruitless. Both María and Alejandra remain enigmas in this frivolous world through which they momentarily pass, and the dialogue which Castel and Martín so assiduously seek ends in failure.

As a result of the interlude in Wanda's *boutique* Alejandra emerges as a more complex figure in the novel. In reality this is only another example of her enigmatic behavior, but coming as it does several months after the beginning of her affair with Martín, it leads him to the very brink of despair and to the threat of suicide. An interesting parallel to Martín's despair is the increasingly serious political chaos in 1955 which resulted in predictions of a national disaster. While Martín seems oblivious to the serious political situation about him, there nevertheless is an increase in such activity throughout the second part of the novel.

One of the frequenters of Chichín's pizzeria, El Loco Barragán, is a key secondary figure in presenting the picture of turmoil characteristic of the period. Considered a crackpot by the other patrons of the establishment, Barragán, half-drunk, preaches wild predictions of a time of vengeance, blood, and fire which will engulf Buenos Aires and bring about the downfall of Perón. Most of his listeners are Peronists who take his predictions with a grain of salt. Martín and Alejandra witness one of his violent tirades, and Martín cannot help but associate his predictions with Alejandra's premonitions of purification by fire.

El Loco Barragán, a fool and the object of ridicule, introduces a theme which is to occupy a significant place in the unfolding of Sábato's message to the readers of *Sobre héroes y tumbas*. While Barragán's words are lost in the laughter of Chichín's patrons, Martín is unable to forget them. They seem inextricably linked with Alejandra's beliefs about the necessity of fire to achieve ultimate purification. In the same scene Barragán shouts that happiness can be found only in the heart, thereby planting another of Sábato's philosophical seeds which is to burst into bloom at the conclusion of the novel. In the next scene following Barragán's tirade Bruno develops the latter idea more completely with his observation that man is not made solely of desperation but also of faith and hope for a better future. Such a deep-seeded faith inspires man to act and to escape from the force of total desperation. Bruno's thoughts continue until he ultimately reaches an Existentialist plane of action: If anguish is the result of man's confrontation with the complete void of nothingness, is not hope the ontological proof of a mysterious moving force behind all existence? In Bruno's mind hope and anguish represent the natural consequences, as it were, of a Supreme Force and of excruciating nothingness; they are proof that both exist. Sábato is always careful not to present God as necessarily the same as the Supreme Force behind life. While never denying that such *may* be the case, he steadily affirms that he is unable to prove or disprove the existence of God. Barragán, however, sees a vengeful God who will sweep down on Argentina with the full force of biblical zeal to cast the wicked into a fiery caldron of brimstone. In this matter Bruno may be considered the spokesman for Sábato, since the author of the holocaust which is soon to engulf Buenos Aires is not at any time identified.

Martín enters the most anguished period of his life near the end of the second part of the novel. The destruction of the world about him and of the intimate world shared by him and Alejandra are concurrent. The beginning of the destruction of the relationship between the two lovers is symbolized by their return to the bar where they experienced their first moments of happiness only to find it permanently closed. Questioning the owner of a kiosk on the corner, they discover that Vania, the owner of the bar, has been interned in an insane asylum. From that moment on their relationship gradually becomes more impossible. It is as if Alejandra has a dragon within her, a dragon which she is unable to describe or conquer. Repeatedly Martín attempts to prolong their relationship, offering to see her on her own terms and at the time and place she might designate. Although continued interviews in Alejandra's opinion would be totally fruitless, she does agree finally to one last meeting at the Adam Bar. This last encounter is even less satisfactory than those which immediately preceded it. Alejandra is lost in another world of thought. Leaving the bar, they walk through the Plaza San Martín overlooking the waterfront. Suddenly, as she has so frequently done in the past, Alejandra announces that she must leave, that she must be elsewhere at eight o'clock. Although Martín desperately shouts at her as she rushes into the night, she continues with an impenetrable look of harshness on her face.

At this point in the novel Sábato introduces Fernando for the first time. Martín follows Alejandra to a small bar where he sees her engaged in an agitated conversation with a dark, sinister figure who seems to emanate a deep feeling of tragedy and horror. Martín cannot help but compare him with a bird of prey, for indeed his hands and face reveal aquiline qualities. At the same time, this unknown man closely resembles someone Martín knows. Suddenly he is struck by the revelation that this is the mysterious Fernando whom Alejandra has mentioned occasionally in the past but whom she has always refused to identify. A flood of ideas quickly engulfs Martín: there is a close resemblance between Fernando and Alejandra's ancestors whose pictures Martín saw the night of his first visit to her home; Fernando must be a relative of Alejandra; furthermore, the two of them are almost certainly in love.

Armed with this new evidence, Martín calls Alejandra and demands another brief interview in which he confronts her with the idea that she and Fernando are relatives and probably lovers who share a remote, secret world. Alejandra reacts violently to Martín's suggestion and shouts back at him that Fernando is her father. Petrified, Martín watches her run into the darkness. Heretofore the idea that Fernando is Alejandra's father has never occurred to Martín, and it is safe to say that few readers would guess the relationship were it not mentioned in the introductory section of the novel. Presented as it is at the midpoint of the novel, this revelation opens up a veritable flood of questions, some of which go back to the first part of the novel and the Barracas fire and the subsequent death of Alejandra and her father. In the first edition of the novel this information is presented in the form of a prologue signed by Sábato. Subsequent editions contain the same information in the form of a police chronicle which ostensibly appeared in *La Razón* on June 28, 1955. Now that the blood relationship between Alejandra and Fernando is clearly established, the many puzzling aspects of their involvement which Alejandra has previously suggested remain in Martín's mind and continue to haunt him.

A feeling of absolute solitude and isolation reminiscent of Juan Pablo Castel seizes Martín del Castillo. It is important for a better comprehension of the Martín-Alejandra relationship to note here that Martín suddenly feels that he has lost a mother. This maternal anxiety goes back, of course, to his early feelings of rejection and explains to a degree his attraction to the older Alejandra. Coupled with these feelings of despair is a certain awareness that the world about him is also tumbling down. Martín's political naïveté has previously been described, but the constant analysis of the situation by Bruno and by the clientele of Chichín's pizzeria could not possibly go completely unnoticed. Likewise he was a pawn in the violence which swept Buenos Aires with the 1955 attack on the Plaza de Mayo and the burning of the principal churches in the capital by elements of Perón's labor unions. Momentarily, Martín must turn his attention to the holocaust swirling about him, and when pressed into service to save some valuable religious objects from destruction, he reacts almost as an automaton. The cold drizzle which comes to hover over the burning city deepens the solitude in which Martín is caught. His confused mind is unable to solve the three-word riddle which incessantly assails him: Alejandra, Fernando, blindness.

A curious scene concludes the second part of *Sobre héroes y tumbas*: in his aimless wandering Martín finally reaches the plaza in front of a church in the Belgrano district of Buenos Aires. He has never been in this area before, and the church is unknown to him. To his great surprise, Alejandra suddenly appears walking resolutely toward a door beside the church. She enters and remains within throughout the night. In the gray dawn Martín finally gives up hope of her leaving the building and reluctantly heads for the heart of the city.

The conclusion of the second part of the novel is as enigmatic as the previous actions of Alejandra. The entire scene is coincidental in every respect, and there is no logical explanation for the encounter of Martín and Alejandra in a spot far from their normal areas of movement. Sábato does not attach any particular meaning to these events, but they do offer a direct path to the "Informe sobre ciegos," Fernando's memoirs which survived the Barracas fire. An analysis of this curious and terrifying document will be the subject of the following chapter of the present study.

CHAPTER 5

An Idiot's Tale

PERHAPS the most enigmatic division of *Sobre héroes y tumbas* is Fernando Vidal Olmos's "Informe sobre ciegos" the strange document which survived the Barracas fire and which Sábato uses as the third part of his novel. The exact relationship of the nightmare which it relates to the other three parts of the novel is not evident after a first cursory reading, but a closer inspection reveals a great deal of thematic unity between it and the other parts as well as numerous instances in which the document clarifies otherwise obscure relationships. Although Fernando ostensibly offers it as a scientific document which he hopes some institute will use to investigate the world of the blind after his death, it is not scientific in any sense of the word. Yet Sábato insists that while it is less than scientific in its method, at the same time it offers the reader insight into a mysterious, hallucinatory world which for Fernando is as real as the distorted world of Juan Pablo Castel in *El túnel*. In *El escritor y sus fantasmas* Sábato admits that Castel prefigures Fernando and that both are obviously victims of a persecution complex which eventually conquers them and leads to their ultimate mental destruction. The parallelism between the two is even more striking when one considers the fact that Castel finally finds himself locked in a tunnel while Fernando ultimately reaches a series of subterranean passages which unavoidably lead to his destruction.

While the incidents of the other three parts of *Sobre héroes y tumbas* are based on historical facts, it is soon evident that the fine line between history and hallucination quickly disappears in the third part, and the reader has no other recourse than to accept the picture of Fernando's world as it filters through his twisted mind. All of the action of *El túnel* was filtered through Castel's mind, but in the second novel the same events are related by Bruno in the fourth part, thereby giving two versions of the tumultuous years from Fernando's birth in 1911 until the fire on June 24, 1955, in which he and Alejandra are destroyed. It is through Alejandra that the historical events of the nineteenth century are presented in the novel, while Fernando and Bruno relate the events of the twentieth century from their individual points of view. Bruno and Martín continue the narrative beyond 1955, although their observations are largely devoted to reminiscence and anguished analysis of past events.

Although much of the "Informe sobre ciegos" takes place in a world of fantasy, the first half of the document could easily be the work of a rational soul given to occasional paranoid tendencies. The reader must arbitrarily decide where Fernando enters the world of the unreal, but a convenient dividing point comes near the midpoint of the "Informe," when in his pursuit of the blind Celestino Iglesias he enters a subterranean passage which leads him to a world populated by abnormal creatures and ruled by a sect made up exclusively of the blind. There is a kind of dichotomy between the events described in the first half of the document and those which take place underground, but in all truth the former lead directly to the latter. When all of Fernando's life is viewed as a unit, it presents a picture of the gradual disintegration of a tormented mind which has had a nefarious effect on all who have come into contact with it.

I *The World of the Blind*

Fernando is in many ways an autobiographical figure. Writing in *El escritor y sus fantasmas*, Sábato indicates that Fernando represents his most unpleasant, "nocturnal" personality (*Escritor*, p. 22). The date of Fernando's birth in Capitán Olmos, June 24, 1911, is the same as Sábato's; and and Capitán Olmos is, by Sábato's own admission, a fictional representation of Rojas. Bruno also was born in Capitán Olmos and therefore has known Fernando from his childhood days. Fernando's physical appearance is more carefully documented in the novel than is the appearance of any of the other three protagonists. The first description of him is near the end of the second part when Martín surreptitiously observes a meeting between him and Alejandra in an obscure café. In the "Informe," all of which is written in the first person, Fernando

minutely describes himself, including such points as his height
and weight. The conclusion that to a degree Sábato was
describing himself is inescapable, but it must constantly be
remembered that Fernando represents only one aspect of his
creator's personality, and that Bruno, Martín, and even
Alejandra are also in one way or another Sábato.

There is no logical explanation for Fernando's obsession
with blindness, which is primarily an extension of Sábato's
interest in the same subject. In response to many queries
concerning this obsession, Sábato explained his own personal
feelings in these words:

> I must confess that I experience a strange and ambiguous feeling in
> their [blind people's] presence, as if I were on the brink of an abyss in
> the midst of darkness. Yes, I feel something on my very skin, some-
> thing I cannot define or explain. And that which I experience in ger-
> minal form I developed to the point of delirium in Fernando's mind,
> and thus I wrote the "Informe." This does not mean that I share
> such madness in the same way or to the same degree. On the other
> hand, I hope you will understand that this is not a scientific or
> literal "investigation," for it is something less and something more
> than that, although if you were to ask me exactly what it is, I
> wouldn't be able to tell you. (*Escritor*, p. 18)

There is a striking parallel between the first chapters of the
"Informe sobre ciegos" and the first three chapters of *El túnel*.
Both are written in the first person, and both begin, so to
speak, after the narrator has experienced the events he is
going to relate. Castel is in prison, and Fernando is hurriedly
finishing his manuscript in an effort to get it into final form
before his death. The line "My name is Fernando Vidal Olmos . . ." immediately recalls to mind the opening sentence of
El túnel, and the fact that both narrators at first seem lost in
the maze of the facts they are attempting to describe indicates
the mental derangement they both suffer at the time they
begin to write. While the two works deal with quite different
material, both are the result of the narrator's obsession, an
obsession which leads Castel into a hermetic tunnel and
Fernando into the labyrinthine sewer system of Buenos Aires.
In a sense neither is able to escape; the fate of Castel is eternal
imprisonment both physically and spiritually, and Fernando
is doomed to immolation.

Indicative of the nightmare that Fernando is to experience is a recurrent dream he has had as a child in Capitán Olmos. In the dream a child, which he later identifies as himself, is playing a game beside a wall which projects a shadow. Gradually the shadow begins to move, but its movement is not the natural result of the earth's rotation. At its approach, Fernando would awake in a cold sweat screaming in terror. As he recalls the dream, he realizes that it was either an indication of the life of terror he was later to live or the symbolic beginning of the terror itself. Through adolescence the dream continued to pursue him, often taking shape during his waking hours. Tormented by this enigma, he even desired internment in an insane asylum so that he would not have to struggle to maintain the difference between reality and fantasy which the world demanded.

The shadow in Fernando's dream is also symbolic of blindness which is the subject of his treatise. Although Fernando affirms that the study is composed of facts as they really occurred, even after reading a few pages one cannot accept this statement at its face value. For Fernando they *are* facts, but for the reader they are the result of an extreme case of schizophrenia. In all fairness, however, one must admit that his investigation begins with three rather normal case histories, the third of which is the well-documented study of Celestino Iglesias, a Spanish Anarchist who became blind in an accident and who ultimately provided Fernando with a key to the world of darkness. Two other figures, Norma Pugliese and Inés González Iturrat, are not directly related to his study of blindness but rather represent the shallow intellectualism so abhorrent to Sábato.

Fernando's investigation of the world of the blind begins during the summer of 1947 when by chance he comes face to face with a blind woman selling trinkets in the Plaza de Mayo. Unimportant in itself, the incident starts a chain reaction in his mind and begins what he calls "the final stage of my existence." On June 14 of the same year another, more frightening incident takes place in the Palermo subway. Fernando has been observing a blind man selling pencils in the crowded subway cars. After making innumerable trips on the same line to observe him, he decides to follow him through the streets when suddenly the blind man steps from behind a corner where he has stopped to await Fernando. Seizing him with one of his powerful arms, the blind man shouts into his ear, "You have been following me." Terrified and nauseated, Fernando stammers that there must be some mistake and flees in the opposite direction. This episode completely unnerves him, but at the same time it convinces him of the existence of a secret sect of the blind, a subworld which he knows he must penetrate.

After a series of digressions regarding the existence of God and the differences between those born blind and those who become blind because of an accident, Fernando reaches the conclusion that the Prince of Darkness, not God, still governs the world and that he governs it by means of the Holy Sect of the Blind. After relating a series of autobiographical details already discussed, Fernando is prepared to describe his first meeting with Celestino Iglesias who ultimately facilitates his entry into this mysterious and horrifying world of darkness.

The Iglesias episode contains a number of elements which are almost certainly autobiographical. The first contact occurs in 1929 in an Anarchist center in the industrial complex of Avellaneda just beyond the city of Buenos Aires on the road to La Plata. At this same time Sábato was a student at the National University of La Plata, and his activities in student political movements are well documented. Although Anarchism was a popular philosophy in Sábato's student days, all indications point to his participation in leftist organizations. There are, nevertheless, many similarities between his activities and those of Fernando who meets Celestino Iglesias through the intervention of a mutual friend. Contrary to the normal Anarchist, Iglesias was a well-mannered, kind individual, a pacifist, and a vegetarian. One might even call him an idealist. A Spaniard by birth, he had spent most of his life in a number of prisons in Spain and Argentina because of his political convictions.

In 1936 Iglesias returned to Spain to participate in the civil war, and Fernando does not see him again until his return to Argentina some years after the conclusion of hostilities. The second meeting is brought about because of Fernando's association with a group of counterfeit agents. Needing someone who could be taken into confidence and who could falsify money, Fernando immediately thinks of Iglesias who now works for a printing establishment. Since the counterfeit money was ostensibly to be used by a Swiss Anarchist group, Iglesias readily agrees to undertake its manufacture. Here again by a strange series of coincidences Fernando is thrown into contact with the world of the blind. In the process of preparing the plates to print the money, Iglesias approaches a Bunsen burner with a tray of acid. Moments before the ensuing explosion which cost him his sight, Fernando has a premonition of what is going to happen. But in any case he now had a new subject for clinical observation in his obsessive investigation.

It is interesting to note that Fernando always gives the appearance of a scientific approach to his study. Earlier in his analysis of the existence of God he developed a series of theorems which covered every possibility which the problem presented. In *El túnel* Juan Pablo Castel engages in a similar analysis of all possible ramifications of the María-Hunter-Allende triangle. In the case of Iglesias, Fernando likewise outlines the four steps he took to effect his study of the case history in point. In the first place it was necessary to pay a sum of money to Iglesias's landlady to make certain that she would report any incident which might be of interest to Fernando. As a second step he convinced Iglesias not to make any decision without consulting him. To protect his scheme even further he spent hours in a café across the street from where Iglesias lived so that every movement through the entrance to the rooming house could be observed. Finally as a cover for his activities and as a means of diversion he entered into relations with the teacher, Norma Pugliese, with the avowed purpose of corrupting her. In all of these cases Sábato's scientific training is readily apparent. Castel and Fernando are not the only characters who analyze their thoughts in this manner; both Martín and Bruno do very much the same thing, although neither reaches the point of numbering the possibilities which a given problem presents.

Within the total structure of the "Informe sobre ciegos" the episode of Norma Pugliese and her professor, Inés González Iturrat, at first seems as unrelated to the problem at hand as the "Informe" has appeared to many critics to be an unnecessary component of the novel. A closer inspection of both sections, however, shows them to be intricately related to Sábato's basic philosophy if not absolutely necessary elements of the larger unit in which they are placed. While Fernando's attempts to seduce the naïve, idealistic Norma Pugliese are included to show his basic drive to conquer and destroy anything representative of the altruistic, at the same time this episode is a vehicle by which Sábato is able to present a summary of the ideas apparent in the first three volumes of essays. Norma's mentor, the corpulent, energetic, masculine Inés González Iturrat, is a defender of the rights of women and of the great progress the world has made due to scientific advances. Fernando, here obviously serving as a spokesman for Sábato, uses Norma's professor as a foil for expounding the basic ideas of *Heterodoxia* and *Hombres y engranajes*. To her affirmation that man and woman are basically the same, Fernando counters with an analysis of the obvious anatomical differences between the sexes. As soon as the professor is able to regain her composure she triumphantly cites the work of Madame Curie and announces the fact that a delegation of North American industrialists which has recently arrived in Argentina includes three women in managerial positions. These statements provide the author with an opening for an attack on the world of reason and science, a topic, heretofore almost absent from *Sobre héroes y tumbas*. Sábato's ideas are not new; he points out that the slave masters of past history are still present in the form of machines which have imprisoned twentieth-century man. Furthermore, he states that the atomic bomb dropped on Hiroshima is no more humane than the bow and arrow used in the Battle of Poitiers. A high level of education and technical advancement does not guarantee a high moral level; Germany of the mid-1930's is a case in point. Fernando also insists that the highly mechanized society of the United States has produced a population two-thirds of which is neurotic.

Inés González Iturrat, furious and at a loss for words, makes a hasty departure, but the entire episode is a disquieting one for Fernando. Why did Norma introduce him to her professor? Is Norma perhaps a spy sent by the blind to follow his movements? While the questions go unanswered, their relationship moves forward to the point that he finally is able to seduce Norma and introduce her to the perverted world of the Marquis de Sade. At this point in the "Informe" the tone changes rapidly to one of Baudelairian concern for the morbid and the repugnant. The mental deterioration of Fernando suddenly becomes more evident as his investigation progresses. The vocabulary is one not usually found even in the Spanish American realistic novel; Fernando is in the midst of a world dominated by evil, which in turn is personified by the Holy Sect of the Blind. An understanding of this point is necessary for comprehension of the paranoid overtones which gradually emerge in this part of the novel.

Fernando's entry into the world of darkness is facilitated by the sudden appearance of a visitor to the rooming house where Celestino Iglesias lives. Although Iglesias's landlady believes that the visitor is an employee of the electric company sent to check her appliances, Fernando suspects that at last a member of the secret sect has come to make an initial contact with Iglesias. The mysterious visitor returns later the same day with a short, fat companion who enters Iglesias's room. From his vantage point across the street in the café, Fernando, in a state of almost unbearable anxiety, awaits some sign of what the visit will produce. After a few moments Iglesias and his visitor leave the rooming house, and Fernando follows them at a prudent distance.

At this point in the narrative the action takes the form of an obsessive pursuit of the unknown which has fascinated Fernando since his investigation first began in 1947. One cannot fail to compare this quest with Castel's pursuit of the unknown girl who seemed to understand the significance of his painting. While Castel temporarily loses María in the crowed streets of Buenos Aires, Fernando is able to follow Iglesias and his companion as they board a bus for Belgrano. During the ride he engages in speculation as to where they are going when suddenly the two move toward the exit and get off at Sucre Street. Again Fernando follows the pair as they move in a mazelike fashion through the streets of Belgrano either in an attempt to confound any possible pursuer or in an effort to disorient the blind Iglesias. Finally they reach the plaza in front of the Inmaculada Concepción church. For a moment it appears to Fernando that they are going to enter the church, and thoughts of a secret liaison between the two institutions fill his mind. But Iglesias and his companion enter the second story of an old house facing the plaza.

An important observation is necessary at this point. In the last chapter of the second part of the novel, Martín has wandered in a daze through the streets the same night of the burning of the churches of Buenos Aires. Purely by chance he reached the Belgrano plaza, a part of the city he has never visited. As he sat on a bench in the plaza in a state of total disbelief, Alejandra suddenly appeared and walked resolutely toward an old house facing the plaza and entered. The plaza is, of course, the same one to which Iglesias and his companion lead Fernando, and there is no reason to doubt that the house they enter is not the same one entered by Alejandra. Furthermore, both events occur at about the same date in 1955 thereby leading to the conclusion that there is a great deal more than coincidence in the fact that Alejandra and Fernando both reach the same plaza in Belgrano at approximately the same time. Alejandra entered the house, apparently the same one entered by Iglesias and his companion. Fernando stays in the plaza awaiting further developments, and at two o'clock in the morning Iglesias and the other man finally leave, locking the door behind them. Fernando is now face to face with the door which may provide him with the secret to all his previous investigations, but it is unmistakably locked. He rouses a reluctant friend to accompany him to Belgrano to pick the lock, and the gates to the unknown stand open before him. It is now too late to retreat, but the open door to the Holy Sect of the Blind is as frightening as if it were the open gate to hell, as indeed it may possibly be. Fernando enters, closing the door behind him.

II *Underground*

Fernando's cloacal journey through the sewers of Buenos Aires can only be interpreted in a symbolic sense. His journey may easily be compared with the evolutionary history of mankind: Fernando alternately becomes a serpent, a fish, and a salamander as he describes his journey through the diabolic labyrinth.[1] The journey begins as Fernando finds a secret door in the floor of the house which leads to the basement from whence he enters a long passage. Apparently the passage terminates in nothingness, but another door comes into view, and behind it there stands a blind woman awaiting him. This is not the first time that an episode in the novel seems planned by some superior force. Alejandra's first words to Martín were that she had been expecting him. One may conclude, therefore, that nothing in Sábato's world is coincidental, that everything is directed by a power at once esoteric and unconquerable. Fernando has no choice but to accept this new reality in which he finds himself. He is so nauseated by the appearance of the blind woman that he falls into a state of spiritual penumbra in which he almost loses consciousness. This mental state is characterized by a series of reveries which are autobiographical in nature but which at the same time describe events in Sábato's own life.

As a prelude to these autobiographical reveries there occurs a scene symbolic of the punishment the sect has in store for him: Fernando is in a boat on a dark, quiet lake when suddenly a flock of birds similar to the ones he knew as a child in Capitán Olmos appears. Bruno later reports that one of Fernando's favorite childhood pastimes was to blind birds and to free them later so that he could observe their desperate flight in total darkness. At the other end of the lake Fernando steps from the boat on to the muddy bank at which point he is attacked by a huge bird which destroys both of his eyes. Symbolically Fernando is now blind himself, but the whole episode is only a part of the dreamworld in which he is a prisoner of the woman sent by the sect to torture and imprison him.

After this episode Fernando finds himself again locked in the room, whereupon he begins to recall details of his life before he entered this subterranean world. A most disquieting thought which comes to disturb him concerns the vengeance brought by the sect on a couple which has tried to escape from the service of a blind man. Years later the revenge came when the couple, now servants in the home of a wealthy family, was imprisoned in an elevator as the family closed the house for the summer holidays, shutting off the electric current as the pair descended. This "accident" was part of a vengeful plan initiated by the sect, and Fernando feels that the gruesome death which awaited the pair trapped in the elevator is not unlike the fate awaiting him in the locked room.

An interesting passage in which Fernando gives his own interpretation of *El túnel* follows. His interpretation differs significantly from that of the critics and from Sábato's as well. The very fact that Fernando sees the crime and subsequent imprisonment of Juan Pablo Castel as a direct result of a complicated plan by the Holy Sect of the Blind to gain revenge for some act committed against them by the well-known painter is evidence enough of the extreme degree of paranoia which he suffers. Allende, María's husband, serves as the key to the crime, although Fernando feels that he may have played an unknowing role in its execution. It was Allende, nevertheless, who indirectly encouraged the relationship by delivering María's letter to her lover and eventual murderer. Although the reasons for the sect's revenge are never clear to Fernando, he dismisses everything as the result of the ambiguous actions of the blind which never do make any sense.

Both of these incidents serve to introduce a rather long autobiographical sketch which covers the years of Fernando's life from 1947 shortly after the incident of the blind man in the Palermo subway until his return years later to Argentina and his subsequent encounter with Celestino Iglesias. Armed with a false passport he decided to leave Argentina, going first to Uruguay where he renewed old acquaintances and frequented the well-known Tupí-Nambá café, long a center for intellectual gatherings in Montevideo. From Uruguay Fernando flew to Paris where he unavoidably came in contact again with representatives of the secret sect. This contact is brought about by his association with the Surrealist painter, Oscar Domínguez, one of the two or three figures in the novel who are not fictional creations.

An important parallel between Fernando's life and that of his creator occurs in the relationship of both to Oscar Domínguez. Some ten years before Fernando's 1947 visit to Paris, Sábato himself had made his second trip to the French capital where he did research in the Curie laboratory. This was a moment of crisis in Sábato's life described in *El escritor y sus fantasmas* in terms which are almost identical to lines written by Fernando in the "Informe sobre ciegos" shortly before his death. Sábato's inner struggle is described in the following manner: "Thus I returned to Paris for a second time. But when I began my duties with Irène Joliot, I suddenly realized that all of this was only a complicated means of evasion and basically a cowardly escape from my authentic interior problems. I began to associate myself with the Surrealists, particularly with Oscar Domínguez, and in that manner I believe that the final (and most authentic) stage of my life began." (*Escritor*, p. 11). Fernando considers his investigation the last stage of his life, and it is through Oscar Domínguez that one of the significant phases of the investigation begins. In a parallel manner the painter introduced Sábato to the more "authentic" world of Surrealism, thereby ending his career in science.

Through Domínguez, Fernando comes in contact with a blind model, and as a result of this association he enters a complex world of the grotesque which only serves to accentuate his persecution complex. Domínguez's passionate, blind model becomes another case history in Fernando's investigation. After secretly observing her several times as she poses for the artist, Fernando discovers certain shocking details concerning her past history. She is married to a blind paralytic whom she hates. An especially severe form of torture which she has devised is to bring her lovers to their apartment where the helpless husband could only emit noises to express his horror as he is forced to listen to one seduction after another.

Even Fernando, who by now is used to the most unimaginable forms of violence, is repulsed by this particular episode. The element which most affects him is the extremely harsh form of persecution to which the model's husband is subjected. At the same time it is apparent that Fernando views this as an extension of his own paranoia. He is, nevertheless, prevented from feeling any true compassion for the blind paralytic since he too forms a part of the sect. Fernando's suspicions are confirmed when he approaches the couple's apartment to keep a date with the model. He hears conversation and concludes that she is entertaining another visitor before she is scheduled to receive him. When he enters at the appointed hour, to his horror he discovers that there is no third person present. The only possible conclusion is that the husband is not a paralytic at all but rather a spy sent by the sect to follow Fernando's every move.

Immediately Fernando leaves Paris, for he is convinced that a vast network is in operation to catch him. This network quite clearly is the result of Fernando's own mental deterioration. As is usually the case in extreme paranoia, the victim feels completely defenseless in a world determined to persecute and torment him. In Fernando's mind nothing happens as the result of coincidence; his association with Domínguez only served to put him in contact with the sect again by means of the blind model. He cites the histories of Maupassant and Gaugin as two other victims of the sect who paid for their interest in the blind with the ultimate loss of their sanity.

In an effort to escape momentarily Fernando goes first to Rome, then to Egypt, to India, to China, to San Francisco, and finally back to Argentina where he was thrown into contact with Celestino Iglesias. The chain of events following his association with Iglesias has already been developed—the accident, his long wait, his entry into the house in Belgrano, and finally his imprisonment in the sealed room presided over by the repugnant blind woman. In much the same way that Sábato's association with Oscar Domínguez served to introduce him to the world of the Surrealists, so does Fernando's contact with him lead to a world which could easily be the creation of a writer or a painter from the same Surrealist group.

Fernando's cloacal journey through the fetid tunnels of Buenos Aires is resumed after the long digression which described his sojourn is Europe and his subsequent trip around the world. Freeing himself from the clutches of his blind guardian, he moves into another room, then through passage after passage, each one more frightening than the previous one. This inferior world must be considered as the subconscious, tormented mind of Fernando. The endless tunnels seem to lead to nothingness in the Existentialist sense of the word. Fernando's desperation is accentuated by the possibility of death at each turn and by the sensation that his body is undergoing a series of metamorphic changes from a fishlike state to more advanced evolutionary forms. In typical Existentialist fashion his journey is all for naught, since he ultimately finds himself again in the sealed room of the blind woman.

At this point in the narrative Fernando is the victim of a veritable avalanche of sensations and feelings. He is, in his own mind, an anti-hero, a kind of king of the underworld. The blind woman, however, is the all-powerful queen of darkness against whom he is completely helpless. She is a representative of the eternal woman in his mind—mother, daughter, lover, and all the forces of evil which woman represents in Fernando's life. A passing reference to Oedipus suggests the psychological relationship between him and his mother, Ana María, a relationship later confirmed by Bruno in the fourth part of the novel. Since Fernando engages in "tenebrous copulation" with the blind woman, there is a clear suggestion that the unnatural relationship extends to his daughter Alejandra as well. The two seem to be travelers in the same underworld, since both were seen to enter the same door in Belgrano at an earlier point in the novel. Alejandra and Fernando are, therefore, classic examples of the complexes suffered by Electra and Oedipus, respectively. Their frightful tale of paternal and maternal fixation is the allegorical "Informe sobre ciegos" in which the blind queen of the underworld comes to represent the women in Fernando's life. Georgina, the cousin who bore Fernando's daughter Alejandra, also fits this same formula when one considers that physically she closely resembled Fernando's mother. The confusion of Alejandra, Georgina, and Ana María into one allegorical figure is therefore not unusual.

A fourth figure represented by the blind woman is death itself. She holds dominion over Fernando from the moment he enters her world as a mysterious voice proclaims to him, "Enter. This is your beginning and your end" (*Héroes*, p. 319). The sojourn underground is, in fact, a representation of Fernando's entire life and of the evolution of life itself. Shortly after the copulation scene and successive metamorphic changes, Fernando suddenly awakes from his nightmare and finds himself in his own room in Villa Devoto. How he escaped from the hands of the sect is unknown, but in any case he fully realizes that his end as predicted in the nightmare is near at hand. The curious thing in all of this is that he knows that he must and will go forth voluntarily to seek his death. It is midnight; his "Informe" is now completed. He must leave, for "she" is expecting him.

There is no explanation offered for this last line of the "Informe sobre ciegos." The indefinite "she" no doubt refers to Alejandra, since it could not mean Ana María or Georgina. It also must mean death, and in the final analysis Alejandra and death represent one and the same person. The exact interpretation of the death of Fernando and Alejandra as described in the introduction to the first edition of the novel is unclear. While there is a direct implication that Alejandra is in some way responsible for the fire, the reader's interest is directed to the "Informe sobre ciegos" which survived the fire and which inspired the author to make an investigation of the whole series of tragic events which surrounds the episode. Sábato establishes the fact that the "Informe" is obviously the work of a psychopath, but he throws doubt on the reliability of the order and cause of the events he has reconstructed, passing them off as an attempt to offer a testimony of some of the problems which have been endured "in this extreme corner of the world during recent times" (*Héroes*, p. 12).

Later editions of *Sobre héroes y tumbas* contain a much shorter introduction in the form of a police report abstracted from the June 28, 1955, edition of *La Razón*. Its contents are quite different from the events described in the introduction to the first edition, and it is in many ways a better key to the interpretation of the complex "Informe sobre ciegos." As a result of a police investigation of the Barracas fire, it was discovered that Alejandra's bedroom had been locked from within, that she first had murdered Fernando with a pistol after which she soaked the room with gasoline and ignited the holocaust.

The police chronicle, in a style typical of the press in Latin America, continues with editorial comment on the significance of the crime. Pointing out that the "Informe" is obviously the work of a paranoiac, at the same time it rejects the earlier hypothesis that the fire was the result of a sudden fit of madness. Sábato's intent in the revised introduction is to focus the reader's interest on Alejandra's role in the crime and on the psychological motivations behind it. As has been indicated in the previous chapter, she was constantly oppressed by feelings of guilt and by an obsession with the "filth" which covered her body. Fernando in a sense was responsible for this, and only with his death could she hope to escape, as it were, from the world of mental darkness. But the murder of Fernando was only the first step in the process; the second and final step was purification. This Alejandra accomplished by fire, the same purifying fire which El Loco Barragán predicted would engulf and save Buenos Aires.

The "Informe sobre ciegos" becomes in the light of this analysis a psychological interpretation of the personalities of Fernando and Alejandra while at the same time clarifying a number of uncertainties concerning the actions of the latter and explaining the nature of the chains which prevented her from engaging in a normal relationship with Martín del Castillo. The psychological filth covering her body is better understood after witnessing Fernando's journey through the mental quagmire described in the "Informe." There is, therefore, sufficient evidence to defend Sábato's decision to include this strange document as the third part of his novel. While the chain of events in the novel would not have been greatly altered by its omission, it does serve the valuable purpose of revealing most of the facts surrounding Fernando's mysterious personality, and it does so through the eyes of Fernando himself just as all of *El túnel* was seen through the eyes of the tormented Juan Pablo Castel.

Alejandra's incestuous relationship to Fernando is also revealed in the "Informe" in allegorical fashion. Although she is not mentioned once in the entire document, she most certainly is one of the several feminine figures superimposed in the creation of the blind goddess of the underworld to whom Fernando is fatally attracted. This goddess also includes Ana María, the mother of Fernando, and Georgina, his cousin. Three possible patterns of incest therefore emerge: father-daughter, mother-son, and cousin-cousin. The latter is a doubly complex relationship because Georgina's close physical resemblance to Ana María perhaps caused Fernando to view her as a mother figure in the same way that Castel viewed María Iribarne Hunter in *El túnel*.

While all of the events in the "Informe sobre ciegos" are presented from Fernando's point of view, they are again related by Bruno in the last part of the novel with additional commentaries which no doubt are Sábato's own views on the matter.

CHAPTER 6

An Unknown God

ALTHOUGH the fourth part of *Sobre héroes y tumbas* begins with the account of the death of Alejandra and Fernando, the center of attention quickly shifts to Bruno Bassán whose long tale covers all but the first eight and the last two dozen pages of this part of the novel. Bruno's tale is the third main plot division, the first two being the story of the tragic love affair of Martín and Alejandra and Fernando's disquieting "Informe sobre ciegos." The novel concludes with a series of intercalated scenes describing incidents in Martín's life following the Barracas fire and the last episodes in the heroic march of Lavalle's troops toward the Bolivian border.

It is readily apparent from this brief summary that the last part of the novel contains elements of three separate and seemingly unrelated themes with the section narrated by Bruno Bassán dominating the whole. In a sense, this part of the novel is a summary and a commentary on the preceding parts, and Bruno's story, while it does reveal new facts about Fernando and the Vidal Olmos family, is a retelling of many of the episodes related in allegoric fashion in Fernando's "Informe." Many readers have asked themselves exactly what Sábato intended to say in this vast, complex novel. If there is a "message," it must be found in the last dozen pages in which Martín del Castillo and the bones of Juan Lavalle find a measure of peace after years of tumult. Separated by more than a century as these two disparate representatives of Argentina are, they both evolve as heroes in the sturggle to find a meaning to life and in a way represent a kind of temporal unity in this constant struggle through the ages.

Paradoxically all of the action described in the first three parts of the novel took place after those events described in the fourth part. The fire and the subsequent discovery of the "Informe sobre ciegos" are related in the introduction to the novel, and the long conversations in which Martín and Bruno reconstruct and analyze the former's affair with Alejandra form the first two parts of the novel, both of which antedate the last scene of the fourth part by some two years. In a like manner Bruno's tale is inspired by the death of Fernando and told, ostensibly to Sábato himself, at a time shortly after the incident occurred. The action of the novel, therefore, moves in both directions from the time of the Barracas fire, and it is safe to say that without this one incident there would have been no reason to write *Sobre héroes y tumbas*. Had not this one crucial event in the lives of the four protagonists taken place, Alejandra, Martín, and Fernando would have continued their aimless pilgrimage, and Bruno would have had no inspiration to recall his years of association with the Vidal Olmos family.

I *Bruno's Tale*

Internal evidence within Bruno's reminiscences indicates that this section of the novel is recounted directly to Sábato by Martín's contemplative friend. In a long passage describing Carlos, one of Bruno's and Fernando's mutual friends, it is mentioned that he was closely associated with certain Anarchist groups in La Plata where Sábato perhaps had an opportunity to meet him. This immediately takes the reader back to the early 1930's when Sábato, as a student at the National University of La Plata, was active first in Anarchist and later in Communist movements in the provincial capital. Like Bruno's friend Carlos, Sábato gradually moved toward communism, thus leading one to conjecture that Carlos represents another example of autobiography in the novel. The fact that all of this information is told directly to the author gives the novel yet another point of view. It accomplishes, among other things, Sábato's desire to place himself and his novel in the midst of the whirlwind of contemporary Argentina, causing many readers to wonder if the entire novel was based on historical facts and real people. To this query Sábato finally responded that the novel is pure invention although the problems it presents are in every respect veracious.

Bruno's chronicle begins with his childhood association with Fernando in Capitán Olmos about 1923, continues with a series of events about 1925 when he again met the Vidal Olmos family in the Barracas district of Buenos Aires, and concludes with an analysis of the period around 1930 when he was associated again with Fernando in Anarchist activities. Although Bruno fleetingly describes additional encounters with Fernando after 1930, the period from 1923 to 1930 forms the core of his narrative. Fernando is the central protagonist of this section, but at the same time important data concerning Ana María, Georgina, Fernando's father, and Bruno himself comes into view. Of equal importance is Bruno's description of the fundamental changes which occurred in the political structure of Argentina with the fall of Yrigoyen and the defeat of liberalism in 1930. In a sense, this chronicle completes the historical panorama of the Argentine nation. The history of the Olmos and Acevedo families covers the colonial, independence, and civil war periods; Bruno extends the narrative to 1930; and with Martín's account of the 1955 insurrection against the Perón dictatorship the historical picture is complete.

As is the case throughout the novel, Bruno's narrative does not follow a strict chronological order. This lack of chronology is intentional; it focuses the reader's attention on the events themselves and permits conclusions to be drawn only after considering the totality of life itself. Interspersed throughout the narrative are comments concerning Fernando which reveal the author's own interpretation of this enigmatic figure who, like the moon, reveals only half of himself to the world. If one may consider the "Informe sobre ciegos" as the revelation of Fernando's dark, hidden side, then with Bruno's account a total picture of Fernando Vidal Olmos emerges.

Fernando was not a person whom one could ever "know" in the normal sense of the word. Although Bruno was physically near him in three or four crucial moments of his life, he knew only a part of his personality. Described both as a monstrous cur and as a lunatic, Bruno preferred to view his madness as an unstable quality in his personality which would dominate him during any moment of crisis. A psychological analysis of this instability reveals it to be an advanced case of paranoia which gradually develops into an advanced state of hallucination and delirium described in his "Informe." An interesting commentary on Fernando's personality is Bruno's affirmation that his is an Argentine variety of madness just as Don Quijote suffers a form of madness that could only be

Spanish. Bruno, speaking here for Sábato, describes Fernando's condition as a relatively common phenomenon among certain descendants of aristocratic, oligarchic Argentine families who live in the midst of the twentieth century but who fail to see, hear, or comprehend the basic changes through which the nation has passed. Fernando represents this decadent class of Argentine society through the Olmos side of his family, but the Vidal side which his father injected into this traditional aristocracy represented a violent and tenebrous vitality which resulted in an explosive, tempestuous nature in his son and later in Alejandra. The volatile, enigmatic nature of Fernando and Alejandra is therefore a product of the marriage of two diverse national strains, and the turbulent result is evident not only in the Vidal Olmos combination but also in a large portion of the national population today. It is a basic error, however, to consider Alejandra or even Fernando for that matter as a symbol of Argentina. Many critics have contributed to this basic error, which Sábato himself finally felt urged to deny (*Escritor*, p. 20). It was the author's purpose to create a type truly representative of the Argentine woman but not to use this type in any way to represent the nation as a whole.

It is a well-known fact that one's psychological pattern is largely determined during the formative years of childhood by a variety of experiences which impress themselves on the nascent personality. In view of this fact, the episodes describing the years in Capitán Olmos, the fictional counterpart of Sábato's native Rojas, are doubly important. Both Fernando and Bruno were born in Capitán Olmos, and Bruno met Georgina, Fernando's cousin, there. Three other relationships of a more important nature emerge from these childhood years: Fernando's dominance of Bruno which was to continue until his death, the love of both Fernando and Bruno for the former's mother, and Fernando's hatred for his father. Although the first relationship may be summarized briefly, this in no way implies that it is unimportant. Fernando dominates the lives of all the protagonists of the novel in one way or another, and it is only with his death that his nefarious influence begins to dissipate, if not to disappear. His dominance of Bruno began when both were children and prevented his establishing a satisfactory relationship with Georgina, whom Bruno also loved. Likewise Fernando's dominance was to prevent Alejandra from developing a normal relationship with Martín many years later.

The role of Ana María, Fernando's mother, is dual in nature. Her son's love for her reaches the point of a psychologically incestuous plane. It is the first such case in the novel and serves as a prelude to Fernando's later relationship to Alejandra. There is no doubt that Fernando's excessive love for his mother was inspired in part by his intense hatred for his father, the repugnant Juan Carlos Vidal. Bruno recalls the elder Vidal with a feeling of complete repulsion, a feeling even shared by Fernando despite the fact that he shared many of his father's less desirable characteristics. But if Fernando ever did love anybody, it most surely was Ana María. Bruno also was in love with her, for being left without a mother at the age of two, it was Ana María more than anyone else in Capitán Olmos who came to represent a mother symbol to him. Any attempt on the part of Ana María to respond to Bruno's maternal love created a violent reaction in Fernando, who even attacked Bruno on several occasions in a fit of jealousy.

Sábato projects the love of Fernando and Bruno for Ana María into later episodes of the novel. Her death brought Fernando to the old ancestral home in Barracas where he became a ward of his grandfather. Georgina, his cousin, and Bebe, the fool who constantly played the clarinet, were children in the same house. In the attic lived Escolástica, the daughter of Bonifacio Acevedo who went mad in 1853 when Rosas's Mazorca threw her father's head into the living room. The same cast of characters which Martín was to meet some thirty years later was introduced to Bruno who had come as a fifteen-year-old student to study in Buenos Aires. It is to Georgina to whom the love of Fernando and Bruno for Ana María is projected. The niece of Fernando's mother, Georgina, conserves many of the physical characteristics of her aunt, thereby inspiring the adolescent Bruno to fall in love with someone who carried on the physical characteristics of the deceased Ana María. Whether Fernando actually loved his cousin is doubtful, but he did father her child, Alejandra. Fernando had previously married a sixteen-year-old Jewish girl with whose mother he had been maintaining an illicit affair. After enjoying the home which the girl's father gave them as a wedding present and after spending a considerable sum of money which he received as a result of the marriage, Fernando abandoned the girl.

Throughout the adolescent years during which Bruno was associated with Georgina the power which Fernando held over her gradually increased. At times she reached a state of near automatism in which her will was completely subservient to Fernando. This Georgina was not the same pleasant child Bruno had first met in Capitán Olmos. There were so to speak, two Georginas, the second very different from the first as the power of Fernando gradually transformed her into a taciturn, servile creature.

The cases of normal parent-child relationships in *Sobre héroes y tumbas* are infrequent. Martín del Castillo hated his mother and was unable to communicate with his father. Bruno was two when his mother died, leading him to transfer his maternal affection to Ana María. Fernando's intense love for his mother is abnormal, and his hatred for his father is as intense as Martín's was for his mother. It is not surprising, then, to discover that Alejandra experienced a similar aversion for her mother, Georgina, who abandoned her before the age of ten. Given the family tendency toward the abnormal, it is quite logical that the negative reaction of Alejandra toward her mother should drive her toward her father, culminating ultimately in their prolonged incestuous liaison. A comprehension of this situation and of Fernando's relations with the opposite sex from the days of his childhood in Capitán Olmos clarifies the symbolism of the blind woman in the "Informe sobre ciegos." She is a compendium of at least three concepts— mother, wife, and daughter represented, respectively, by Ana María, Georgina, and Alejandra.

When one considers that Alejandra, while sharing many of the violent personality traits of her father, closely resembled her mother and in turn her grandmother Ana María, another aspect of the incestuous relationship emerges. In a sense, the whole affair is a projection in Fernando's mind of his original sickly love for his own mother. It has already been established

that once Ana María was dead Fernando shifted his fixation
to Georgina, the person who most closely resembled her. With
the virtually complete disappearance of Georgina when Alejandra was about ten, the fixation was then transferred to his
own daughter. One psychological footnote remains in this
whole complicated affair. Bruno in his tale confesses to Sábato
that he too went through a period of infatuation for Alejandra
until he finally realized that he had transferred his impossible love for Georgina to her daughter. Bruno, of course, was
in a position to enter into a normal relationship with Georgina
had it not been for the inhibiting power which Fernando held
over her.

Bruno's tale explains for all practical purposes the complex
web of personal relations which the first three parts of the
novel present. He identifies the "dragon" within Alejandra
which doomed her affair with Martín to utter frustration;
he unravels the confusing allegory in the "Informe sobre ciegos"
and reveals a great deal of his own role in the Vidal Olmos
tragedy. In the last half of his tale the emphasis shifts to a recounting of the political and economic turmoil which swept
over Argentina about 1930. Bruno was caught up in these
heady events through his association with Fernando and with
several of Fernando's acquaintances, all of whom were active
in an Anarchist band seeking to destroy the established social
structure.

The importance of Bruno's relation of the events surrounding
1930 should not be discounted. Sábato himself has analyzed
the fundamental importance of these basic changes which this
year brought about in the following statement: "Here there
are only two or three great events which mark literary movements in my opinion; for example, the end of liberalism about
1930, a period which lasts from that time until today. It is a
period of crisis or rather of hard, problematic judgment."[1]
The beginning of this period was witnessed by Sábato as a
student in La Plata and by Bruno who again was thrown into
contact with Fernando Vidal Olmos.

These were dramatic years. The vividness of the picture
painted by Bruno can be explained by the fact that many of
the events he describes were experienced by Sábato himself.
Bruno's gradual attraction to communism and his subsequent

disenchantment are autobiographical details of Sábato's own youth. Bruno's statement that as a child he was sent to study in a large city far from Capitán Olmos where he was alone, timid, and the victim of a tender sensitiveness recalls an almost identical statement made by Sábato about himself in *El escritor y sus fantasmas* (pp. 9-10). Both Sábato and Bruno witnessed the fall of the society into which they had been born—the collapse of Wall Street and the resultant worldwide economic chaos, the universal crisis in industry, and the downfall of a world built on the premise of reason and scientific progress.

Two case histories are used to describe the turbulence of the day, the histories of Carlos and Max Steinberg. Carlos is a link in the invisible chain by which Bruno again came into contact with Fernando. Through Carlos he became closely acquainted with Max, and through the association of this pair with a group of Anarchists Bruno was unavoidably led into another series of contacts with Fernando. Anarchism was a movement ideally suited to Fernando's destructive personality, for it was not due to any political conviction that he came into the movement. In fact, his penchant for violence so repulsed Carlos that he finally left the movement to become a Communist. Max Steinberg came from a Jewish family whose history went back to the revolutionary movement of Czarist Russia. Max's mother, however, was born in Switzerland and came to Argentina where she studied medicine shortly after her marriage. Fernando's friendship with Max was inspired in part by the attractiveness of the latter's mother, and Bruno finally discovered that they were engaged in a clandestine relationship. This was not the last time that Fernando was to engage in an affair with an older woman; his first marriage to a young Jewish girl also came about after a prolonged affair with her mother.

Bruno's chronicle continues with an explanation of how Fernando, through his Anarchist activities, first met Celestino Iglesias. The narrative ends shortly after that encounter, but the "Informe sobre ciegos" continues the story of Fernando up to the point of his death. Bruno ends his story at the time of the fall of Hipólito Yrigoyen and the end of both liberalism and Anarchism in Argentina. With the termination of these movements came the end of a way of life and a fundamental change in the political orientation of Argentina, a change whose end is not yet in view.

Two incidents near the conclusion of Bruno's chronicle closely link it with the "Informe sobre ciegos" and *El túnel*. The first, a confused dream which Bruno has at the time when the police are seeking to destroy the Anarchists' organization in Buenos Aires, ends with the comment that this dream is the result of his participation in a series of dangerous, perplexing events. Bruno has just moved to another boarding house to escape possible arrest, and as he awakens in the unfamiliar surroundings, he is overcome by feelings of isolation and hopelessness which the new order of things has brought about. Fernando, a much more unstable person than the contemplative Bruno, was led into a hallucinatory world by these same events as witnessed in his "Informe." In sum, both Fernando and Bruno report many of the same events in their respective narratives, but the former so distorts the normal course of these details that one must read Bruno's tale to comprehend fully the significance of the "Informe."

Following his dream, Bruno arises, opens the window of his room, and views the indifferent city below. This scene may be compared with the scene near the end of *El túnel* when Juan Pablo Castel viewed a cold, indifferent Buenos Aires from the window of his cell. The degree of desperation is the same; the only difference is that Castel feels hermetically sealed off from the world as indeed he is for all practical purposes. Bruno is free to leave his room and wander through the streets, which he does, although the possibility of arrest for his association with the Anarchists still exists.

Once outside his room, Bruno views the world about him and fails to see any evidence of the impending revolt of the masses which his leftist and Anarchist books have reported. He is assailed by grave doubts that the social changes he has come to accept as necessary and inevitable are really desired by the masses who seem content to sit on the park benches and watch the hours pass. The answer to Bruno's doubts does not come until much later: "It was many years before I understood that in those same streets, plazas, and even in those stores and offices of Buenos Aires there were thousands of people who thought or felt more or less what I felt at that moment: desperate and solitary people, people who thought about the sense and senselessness of life, people who had the sensation of seeing a dormant world about them, a world of hypnotized people or people changed into automatons" (*Héroes*, p. 388).

Bruno speaks here for the author of *Hombres y engranajes*, for just as Juan Pablo Castel is the victim of a world based on reason, Bruno is an isolated voice of protest in the cold world of the machine. Bruno's protest, however, comes only in the form of a commentary, since by his very nature he is a man of thought and not a man of action. This characteristic of his personality must be understood to comprehend his role in the novel. Sábato has frequently been accused of creating weak masculine characters in *Sobre héroes y tumbas*. While it is true that, except for Fernando, Martín and Bruno seem somewhat colorless and at times abulic, it was Sábato's intention to paint them in this manner as representative victims of the mechanized world in which they live.

Bruno continues to theorize on the meaning of existence with an evolutionary analysis of the development of man. This is not unlike the evolutionary changes of Fernando from a fish to higher forms of life as he progresses through the sewers of the underworld. Bruno carries the process higher as the first primate rises on two feet, passes through the stone age, learns to use fire and the ax, and finally devotes himself to science and technology. The modern urban metropolis is the ultimate result of this mad race in which man gradually divorces himself from zoological happiness. Coming as this summary does near the end of *Sobre héroes y tumbas*, it may be considered a recapitulation of Sábato's ideas previously expressed in the earlier essays and in both of his novels. All of his protagonists in one way or another are victims of the complexities of mechanized urban life. Some, like Castel and Fernando, make solitary escapes into tunnels of isolation. They are extreme cases. Others, like Martín, Bruno, and even Alejandra, seek—sometimes unsuccessfully—to work out a *modus vivendi* with which to confront the world. Alejandra finally chooses self-destruction and murder as a means of solving her struggle. It must be remembered, however, that she also suffers another malady, one inherited from the peculiar circumstances which created her unique family tree. This is again evidence of the fact that Alejandra is a person and not a symbol of the nation in which she was born.

Bruno's solution to life is passive. Possibly because of this, he is often regarded as the least successfully presented of the four protagonists. He does, nevertheless, express some of Sábato's best-known ideas, although Fernando and even Martín also express many of his opinions and grave doubts. As for Martín's solution to the problems which confront him at almost every turn, the reader must wait until the end of the fourth part of the novel where this is clearly expounded and offered as Sábato's own solution to the enigma of life, which his essays and novels have thoroughly described.

II *A Philosophy of Hope*

The last twenty-odd pages of *Sobre héroes y tumbas* are an artful juxtaposition of the final episodes of Lavalle's march toward Bolivia and the events in the life of Martín del Castillo following the Barracas fire in 1955. Sábato's resumption of the Lavalle story and the fact that a great part of it is a repetition of details already presented in the first part of the novel lead to the conclusion that the author intended this historical segment to represent, among other things, a kind of recurring fugue. The Lavalle episode, while depicting heroes and noble deeds of the past century, also serves as a contrast to twentieth-century heroes or the lack of same. As will later be indicated, there is a good case for comparing Lavalle and Martín as heroes on quite different planes and in different circumstances. A kind of historical continuity or substratum is established by the Lavalle segment, since both Fernando and Alejandra are direct descendants of participants in the nineteenth-century drama, and Martín and Bruno through their association with the Vidal Olmos family are thrown into the same historical current.

In the first part of the novel Martín is thrown into contact with the Lavalle episode on the night of his first visit to Alejandra's home in Barracas. At that time he viewed these events as remnants from a distant and remote past which acquired an even greater degree of antiquity as they came from the mouth of Pancho, Alejandra's great-grandfather. Fol-

lowing the fire, Martín returns to the charred remains of the
house where he had known both the greatest ecstasy and the
most overpowering desperation. As he enters the room once
occupied by Pancho and views the old lithographs, fragments
of the last desperate days of the march are to alternate with
Martín's own anguished search for a key to the meaning of
the tragedy and to the meaning of life itself. Lavalle continues
his march because he has hope that the governments of Salta
and Jujuy will join with him in a strong counterattack against
the advancing Federalists. Without this hope there would be
no reason to continue the long march. On the other hand,
Martín del Castillo is without any hope and, for all practical
purposes, without a goal itself. Lavalle has a sense of duty to
his followers in the north whom he cannot abandon even in
the face of overwhelming odds, what with the gradual deser-
tion of many of his own troops.

Both Lavalle and Martín in one sense are on a journey.
Lavalle's destination is apparent, but for the moment Martín
is reduced to a series of disconnected wanderings from one
part of Buenos Aires to another. Momentarily he is reminded
of a less pleasant episode in his association with Alejandra
when he meets her sometime lover, Bordenave. The two have
no common ground for communication, and the interview
serves only to stir up memories which should have remained
buried. Martín finally reaches his miserable room where in his
deepest anguish he seeks some sign which will confirm the
existence of God. Where was God when Alejandra became lost
in a world of wickedness? Why would God permit such trag-
edies to occur? His search for meaning in life is finally reduced
to a demand that if God exists, He must give him, Martín,
some sign, some confirmation.

Martín's search for proof of God's existence has one more
aspect; if the evidence does not appear by the following morning, he will kill himself. Once Martín has established the limits
of the game he will play with God, a whole series of doubts
assails him. His body is momentarily paralyzed, leading him
to the conjecture that he is experiencing a religious stupor,
but if this is God's sign to him, it is ambiguous. Martín fears
that even if God does send him a sign, he will fail to perceive
or comprehend it. There is no other recourse but to leave his

room and walk through the streets again until the deadline set for God's appearance has come or until that time when He shall appear.

One may consider that Martín has reached the lowest point of despair when he leaves his room to walk the streets for what he believes will be his last night. His mind receives the impressions from the lights and sounds about him, but moments later he finds himself on a swampy plain among cadavers and waste. There is an obvious relationship between this scene and the last half of Fernando's "Informe sobre ciegos." It is not unlike Bruno's dream in 1930 which was a confused repetition of the chaotic events of the time. Thus Martín joins the other protagonists, all of whom spent their season in darkness, but only in the case of Fernando did the hallucinatory world finally blot out the real one. Fernando's world of darkness was ruled by the repugnant blind woman. There are, however, some major differences: the female figure in Martín's dream is a real woman who awakens him from his reverie with calm, maternal reassurance. Like Fernando, Martín finds himself in the woman's humble room, decorated with pictures of Carlos Gardel and Eva Perón, but there is no suggestion that he is a prisoner as was the case with Alejandra's father. Martín notes the distinctive accent of the province of Santiago del Estero in her speech, and after glancing about the room for a moment, he hears the cry of an infant. Too weak to attempt to see the child, he falls again into his dreamworld.

At this point Martín again dreams that a beggar approaches him, opens his pack, and speaks words which he is unable to comprehend. This is the third and last occurrence of the same dream in the novel, and each time it occurs it is keyed to Martín's quest for an answer to the enigma which life presents. Here it is directly related to his search for some sign of the existence of God, some proof that the Supreme Being is cognizant of his human needs. The fact that the contents of the beggar's bundle are anonymous and his words are unintelligible indicates that Martín must not expect to unravel the mystery surrounding God and human life, but it does *not* indicate that God does not exist. The very appearance of the beggar is some kind of sign that someone is aware of Martín's problems.

When Martín finally awakes, the surroundings in which he finds himself come into clear focus. He is indeed in a humble home with two other people, a mother and her child. The woman, one Hortensia Paz, has nursed Martín after he was found almost unconscious in the street. During his delirium Hortensia has learned a great deal about him, and in consideration of these facts she offers him words of wisdom which serve as an answer to his quest for God and for meaning in life. There is, according to Hortensia, no reason to despair; life is filled with so many beautiful things. She, for example, has her child—but no husband is apparent—her old phonograph and some of Gardel's tangos, her flowers, her birds, and several dogs. In short, Hortensia is so enthusiastic about life and living that her contagious optimism pierces Martín's despair and inspires him to give her a ring which his grandmother had given him on the occasion of his first communion. Her reluctance to accept the ring is broken when Martín counters with her own philosophy: her acceptance of this token will give him his only moment of happiness in recent days.

There is obvious symbolism in Hortensia's surname, Paz, which comes to represent the first moment of peace which Martín del Castillo experiences after the death of Alejandra. Without a doubt this one person whom he met ever so briefly changed the course of his life and quite possibly saved him from suicide. Name symbolism is not commonly found in *Sobre héroes y tumbas* except for this readily apparent instance. One may conclude that Sábato did not want to risk the possibility of the reader's missing the importance of Hortensia's message. While she in no way represents God Himself, she does reveal to Martín the necessity of observing His presence in the little things of life. At the same time, the fact that she cares whether Martín lives or dies is likewise important to him. That his death would sadden one among the millions of residents of Buenos Aires is enough to give him a reason to live. Hortensia would be enough to cause him to want to live; even the love of a faithful dog would suffice. Also there was his friend, Humberto J. D'Arcángelo. As Hortensia had said, life is full of so many wonderful things that the thought of eventual death is enough to sadden one.

Martín now has a reason for living as did Juan Lavalle whose death is reported in a popular *vidalita* which interrupts the Hortensia Paz episode. Lavalle's sense of duty has finally been comprehended by Martín, who recalls words once spoken by Bruno concerning the need to belong to some group, even if it is nothing more than a company of firemen, and the need to feel a sense of duty and loyalty to a common cause. Implicit in all of this is an adamant rejection of a mechanized society based on a foundation of science and reason. In such a society the individual is little more than a gear in the Great Machine, an *engranaje* as described by Sábato in his earlier essay. Curiously enough Martín and his companion Bruno, both invisible faces among the masses, are the only protagonists in Sábato's novels who reach any kind of solution to the problems they face. Juan Pablo Castel and Fernando are driven to madness by the course of events; María Iribarne Hunter and Alejandra are never seemingly able to solve the mysteries which life has dealt them. It is left to a distraught adolescent and his mature friend to discover ways to cope with the problems which Sábato first posed in *Uno y el universo*.

Hortensia Paz serves the purpose of putting Martín back on the road to life, but if he is to profit from his experience with her, he must begin his journey again, this time with some positive goal in mind. Martín's long-standing desire to visit Patagonia comes to his mind as a suitable destination for the new direction his life is to take, and his old friend Bucich offers a means by which he may reach his goal. Bucich is one on the most refreshing figures in the entire novel. A kind of man of the open road, he drives his truck the three thousand kilometers from Buenos Aires to the Strait of Magellan. The son of a sailor-turned-gold-prospector, Bucich knows Patagonia like the back of his hand. His philosophy of life is not unlike that of Hortensia Paz; he is totally self-sufficient and content with his role in life. As Martín helps him make camp for their first night out of Buenos Aires, he feels useful for the first time in many months. The sense of belonging, which Bruno had earlier described, is finally comprehended by Martín in the wide-open spaces of the pampa.

An interesting factor in Martín's regeneration is the fact that he has to leave Buenos Aires before the final stages of the process can be accomplished. Patagonia works its spell on his sickly soul, and the pure cold air of the desolate stretches gives him new vigor. Martín had always thought of the virgin wasteland of Patagonia as a place where his soul might find release from the maelstrom of the capital. There is a close relationship here to the theme of purification which was introduced earlier in the novel. Alejandra spoke of this need as did El Loco Barragán. Alejandra's concept of purification was a very real personal need, while Barragán predicted a turbulent fate for Buenos Aires if the city did not reject its wicked past. In both cases fire is the cleansing agent: the Barracas catastrophe was an attempt to destroy the filth which Alejandra vainly sought to wash from her body, and the burning of the churches of Buenos Aires during the last months of the Perón dictatorship was the fulfillment of Barragán's prophecy.

As Argentina's last frontier, Patagonia has been considered by many as a possible solution to the nation's economic problems. Rich in petroleum, minerals, and stock-breeding potential, its ultimate development quite possibly would inject a new vitality into an economy which has rapidly declined since World War II. The fact that Martín heads south under the protection and tutelage of Bucich is probably not just an accidental choice on the part of the author. The example of Martín may well be worthy of national emulation.

In contrast to Martín's journey to Patagonia is the trek of the last remnants of Lavalle's legion north to the Bolivian border. Although only the great leader's bones make the last few miles of the journey, the determination of his followers is in no way reduced. By cleverly alternating scenes, Sábato effectively draws the reader's attention first to Patagonia and then to the north. This technique gives the final scenes of the novel a spirit of national as well as historical unity. The same technique is used in the first part of the novel, and its recurrence at the end serves to give a certain measure of plot unity to what otherwise would seem like four hundred-odd pages of loosely related episodes.

There is among the ranks of Lavalle's legion a figure who is in many ways the counterpart of Bucich. He is Aparicio Sosa, a taciturn, dark, pock-marked sergeant who was one of the fallen general's most loyal supporters.[2] It is to Sosa that La-valle's precious bones are entrusted just as Martín in a way is delivered into the hands of Bucich. Both Sosa and Bucich as well as Hortensia Paz are representatives of the common people, the "invisible faces" from which Argentina must draw its strength for the future. Strangely enough, it is through these secondary figures that the protagonists eventually find a way of life, so to speak. Their simple philosophy of life con-sists of an intense loyalty to the small circle of human beings who are in some way dependent on them and to the role as-signed them in the vast drama of life. Above all else they are true to themselves and to those who come in contact with them.

At the conclusion of the novel Lavalle's remains and the last stragglers of his once great legion cross the border into Bolivia. A part of Lavalle is still with them, but the flesh from his bones is flowing back to his native soil to be reincarnated both physically and spiritually as a new Argentina someday emerges. Among those who finally reach safety in Bolivia are Aparicio Sosa, the final guardian of the general's remains, and the young ensign, Celedonio Olmos, who is one of the pro-genitors of the Olmos Acevedo family. As Sosa, Olmos, and the other troops look back to the south, they ask themselves the same question: When will the United Provinces of the South truly achieve unity? Rosas is still in full command, and only scattered forces of resistance remain to challenge him. The tone of Sábato's prose is very much the same as that ex-pressed by Domingo Faustino Sarmiento at the end of *Facundo*. The assassination of Lavalle in 1841 precedes the writing of *Facundo* by only four years, and it was not until 1852 that Rosas was finally defeated. The Unitarians could only hope for the ultimate defeat of Rosas during the bitter years before the Battle of Monte Caseros, and in the hearts of Lavalle's followers it was the memory of their hero's valor that kindled the fire of their resistance until liberation finally came. In no way could Lavalle's sacrifice be considered in vain, for in death as in life he was truly a hero; his journey toward Bolivia was a journey toward eternal consecration.

On a very personal plane Martín's journey to the south is equally productive. While it does not reach the dramatic level of Lavalle's march, it does serve to introduce him to a way of life in the midst of a period no more propitious than was the period of the Rosas dictatorship. The fact that Lavalle's march and Martín's journey both take place during periods of dictatorship and national unrest is important, but it is equally important to note that while the former was intimately involved in national affairs, Martín is only marginally affected by the Perón regime.

On the way to Patagonia that first night, Martín begins to feel the full effect of the change in his life which began with the Hortensia Paz episode. Bucich's devotion to his work and to those who consider him their friend is enough to show him the meaning of Hortensia's message. Bucich's words, "How great is our country . . . ," words spoken beneath the star-studded sky of the pampa, summarize a potential if not an actual truth, and they are enough to make Martín feel that his journey to Patagonia is already worthwhile.

A certain hopeful optimism pervades this fourth and last part of *Sobre héroes y tumbas*. Such a feeling is totally absent from *El túnel* as well as from the first three parts of the novel in question. Sábato, writing in *El escritor y sus fantasmas*, recognizes this fact and explains it in the case of the first novel as the result of youthful disillusion with the current national and international turmoil. While this basic negativism was to continue in *Sobre héroes y tumbas*, reaching its most violent expression in the "Informe sobre ciegos," Sábato could not feel content with the matter until the last section of the novel was finally written and published. Had some catastrophe prevented the appearance of this section, Sábato would have been judged by posterity on the sole basis of his totally negative vision of life. His novelistic goal of explaining to the world what he expects of life and existence would have been unfulfilled. In a sense, then, *Sobre héroes y tumbas* closes a cycle in Sábato's literary production. He has gone through the whole gamut from despair to a kind of cautious hope in the future of mankind, a hope already evident in nascent form in the essay, *Hombres y engranajes*. Many of his questions, however, are still unanswered, and the reading public must await another book or essay to pursue this common quest for an explanation of the riddle of life.

CHAPTER 7

In Search of Ernesto Sábato

EVEN after examining the essays and novels of Ernesto Sábato, a cogent definition of him as a contemporary literary figure remains elusive. There is, however, ample evidence to indicate that the key to the mystery lies buried in his writings, especially in his prose fiction, described by Sábato himself as a suitable source for investigating and defining his literary personality. Germane to the problem at hand is a consideration of Sábato's own concept of twentieth-century literature and the role of the contemporary novel in determining its course. It is necessary at the same time to summarize the literary movements and writers which have influenced Sábato's concept of Western man, the avowed protagonist of all his writings. Finally, it is the essays and the novels themselves which reveal the man to his readers, but this revelation only comes arduously as the result of a good deal of reflective and meditative analysis. Sábato is not an easy or a pleasant novelist to read; his most common themes—incest, blindness, insanity, arson, and abnormal psychology—are not suitable fare for the casual reader seeking light entertainment. But for the reader with an abiding interest in the problems of modern man in an inhospitable world, he has a message filled with despair yet tempered with a small but highly significant measure of hope. In the same way that his view of life, especially in *Sobre héroes y tumbas*, is given from a multiplicity of vantage points, so is his style one which employs a vast number of techniques to achieve the end result.

There is in Sábato's opinion only one kind of valid literature; it is an anguished literature posing the eternal questions concerning the identity of man, his destiny, and his role in the confusing events of his age. Literature is a hybrid expression of the human spirit which lies somewhere between art and pure thought, somewhere between fantasy and reality. Sábato goes on to say that literature more than any other form of art is capable of offering a profound testimony of the crisis in which man finds himself entangled. Literature must be an expression of this complex crisis, or it will be of no value.

In *El escritor y sus fantasmas* Sábato offers a more extensive definition of the contemporary novel which is important as a foundation for the final analysis of his own two novels (pp. 85-89). He takes a determined stand against those who would subject the novel of the twentieth century to nineteenth-century standards. The contemporary novel simply is not interested in the so-called objectivity of the Realists. Its point of departure is man himself, and the immediate goal is the comprehension of the mysterious circumstances which surround man's existence. As man probes within himself Sábato believes that he must discard conventional attitudes regarding time in favor of a kind of personal time measured in moments of despair, happiness, pain, and anguish. Inevitably the contemporary novel must deal with the subconscious, and unless the reader views such events in terms of the laws governing the subconscious, he will reach the equivocal conclusion that he is in a world of fantasy. The world of the subconscious, at least for the individual involved, is just as real as the exterior world in which he moves. Juan Pablo Castel and Fernando Vidal Olmos are two excellent examples of Sábato's penetration of this subconscious world.

The "illogical" episodes described in Fernando's "Informe sobre ciegos" are illogical only in terms of the laws imposed by the exterior world. By the standards of the zone in which they occur, they are in every sense logical and predictable. Castel's journey through life's tunnel is equally logical in terms of the world in which it takes place. In both of these cases the protagonist and the setting are not divorced one from the other as in the case of the nineteenth-century novel, but rather the setting evolves from the individual along with his feelings and ideas. One immediately becomes aware of the many points of view which any incident may elicit, and the problem of communicating these ideological differences becomes critical. Here the fundamental solitude of the individual accentuates this problem and results in the well-known preoccupations with death, hope, absurdity, isolation, and desperation which the Existentialists and their followers so diligently explore. In sum, the twentieth-century novel of Sábato and of many like him has acquired a metaphysical dimension unknown in the novel of the preceding century. This dimension is not the product of a natural evolutionary process but rather the result of a severe crisis in a world which placed all its money on a future based solely on reason and scientific progress. Without a spiritual crisis this fundamental change would not have occured; it is very similar to the situation of a sinking ship which causes the passengers to leave their frivolity to face the greatest problems of their existence which were all the while latent in their normal daily lives.

As a novelist fundamentally concerned with the fate of man and with an analysis of man himself, Sábato joins a lengthy procession of other writers preoccupied with similar problems. A listing of these writers provides one with a view, as it were, of Sábato's literary family tree. At various points in his essays he makes references to his literary ancestors, but a compendium of all those mentioned would fill many pages. There are, however, frequent references to Russian literature and especially to Fyodor Dostoevsky who more than any other Russian left his mark on the author of *El túnel* and *Sobre héroes y tumbas*. Dostoevksy's *Notes from Underground* influenced Sábato greatly with its rejection of petty bourgeois values and its penetration into a world where conventional reason and logic were nowhere to be found. Here is the seed which Sábato was to nurture into *El túnel* and Fernando Vidal Olmos's "Informe sobre ciegos." Even the attempts to remove the shrouds from Alejandra's enigmatic personality and the almost endless soul-searching of Martín and Bruno are part and parcel of this same current.

In general Sábato finds many points of contact between the literature of tsarist Russia and that of Argentina, owing principally to a great similarity of social and economic problems. There also are, in his opinion, close parallels between Russia and Spain, both of which are on the periphery of Europe where no true Renaissance took place. In many of Spain's former colonies, and especially in Argentina, many of these characteristics were accentuated. The society described by Tolstoy with a few minor changes could easily depict life on the vast *estancias* of the pampa. The physical similarity between the steppes and the pampa is only one factor in this relationship; other factors are a similar degree of social disorganization, a pre-capitalistic economy, a patriarchal family system, and a great deal of revolutionary political activities which eventually terminated in anarchism and socialism.

Romanticism in literature and Marxism in politics were to continue this emphasis on man's individuality, although neither movement ever reached the inner metaphysical plane seen in the literature of the twentieth century. Marcel Proust is an example which clearly demonstrates the twentieth-century novelist's attempt to capture reality by means of an anguished appraisal of the inner world of the writer. In the case of Proust it is stimuli from the exterior world which bring a flood of memories from the depths of the subconscious; the world of Proust is re-created from within his own soul just as the world of Sábato's protagonists comes from within them. In *Hombres y engranajes* Sábato expands the list of those contemporary writers who have attempted to define reality from the point of view of the protagonists, and in the light of the present study there is every reason to add the name of Sábato to the list. There are excellent grounds for comparing the monstrous psychological transformation of Juan Pablo Castel and Fernando Vidal Olmos with the physical transformation of Gregor Samsa into a monstrous vermin in Kafka's *The Metamorphosis*. Virginia Woolf's attempt to represent the subconscious aspects of behavior through symbols and interior monologues which delve into the characters' inner selves marks her as another forerunner of Sábato. Other sources may be found in Joyce's interior monologue and especially in the novels of William Faulkner in which each of the figures offers his own perspective of reality. Sábato's concept of inner reality is perhaps best summarized by his quotation from Julien Green that writing a novel is in itself a novel in which the author is the hero, and if he pretends to achieve any degree of objectivity, it is because he is either a novice or a fool, since man can never escape from himself (*Escritor*, p. 81).

Sábato's close relationship to the Existentialists, especially to Sartre and Camus, has already been clearly indicated. It is sufficient here to summarize this liaison in terms of the movement's profound interest in the plight of the individual, faced as he is by the absurdity of the world and the omnipresent menace of death. Existentialism as a philosophical movement was closely related to the destruction of traditional values which World War I brought about, and the turbulent political situation in Argentina after 1930 created fertile ground for the movement to flourish on the banks of the River Plate.

Within the frame of Argentine literature Ernesto Sábato occupies a significant place in the contemporary scene, but it is for future generations to judge the role he will ultimately play in the continuum of River Plate letters. Much of the Argentine literature of the nineteenth century has little in common with Sábato's exploration of the human soul. His rejection of Realism includes most of the figures who wrote after 1880 although he does see great value in José Hernández's classic gaucho epic, *Martín Fierro*, which went beyond the narrow limits of the picturesque to explore the hopes, contradictions, and anguish of the protagonist. This consideration of universal qualities gives Hernández's work a level of importance rarely found in others who cultivated gaucho literature.

The literary generation which immediately preceded Sábato's time was the result of the superposition of waves of European immigrants on the semifeudal structure of twentieth-century Argentina. This resulted in the emergence of two distinct literary currents shortly after World War I. The first of these currents was aristocratic in nature, often seeking its inspiration in French letters. Symbolic of this group's orientation was the elegant Florida Street, which came to be considered as the group's unofficial center. Among its most important figures were Ricardo Güiraldes, the author of the gaucho classic, *Don Segundo Sombra*; Victoria Ocampo, founder of the review *Sur*, which published many of Sábato's early essays and the first edition of *El túnel*; and the well-known contemporary figure, Jorge Luis Borges.

Other writers of a more plebeian persuasion considered social and economic problems in the nascent industrial society of Buenos Aires and its environs. These figures were, in large measure, either children of immigrants like Sábato or native Argentines sympathetic to the plight of the working class. Most representative of this current was the novelist, Roberto

Arlt, and Boedo Street, located in an industrial district of the capital, was the symbolic home of this group. In the critical atmosphere which followed the fall of liberalism in 1930, the generation of which Sábato is the leading figure was born. This new generation is composed of authors grouped together because of a similar spirit of their times, a *Zeitgeist*, and according to Sábato himself it is in no way related to their chronological age or to the secondary events of the period since 1930.[1] Sábato goes on to say that when the contemporary period is reconsidered a century from now, more similarities will be found between him and Roberto Arlt of the Boedo group than with many writers closer to him chronologically. His orientation is much closer to the Boedo group in almost every respect, and he is adamant in his rejection of ludicrous literary preciosity as practiced by some members of the Florida group and their emulators.

Borges as the mentor of the Florida school often seeks his nation's reality in its streets, its patios, and in the boroughs of Buenos Aires. Literary critics have consistently pointed out the many ways in which he and Sábato differ, always failing to identify their common preoccupation with a definition of Argentina and with an analysis of the individual's role in the nation and in the world. Sábato affirms this kindred spirit by stating that "we both are truly Argentine . . . and I believe that we represent two branches of the national spirit."[2] Both view their country and its inhabitants somewhat in the same manner as did the Generation of 1898 in Spain. Their own suffering as they investigate the unhappy details of the reasons behind Argentina's present condition is a reflection of the suffering of both the intelligentsia and the common man of their nation today. Considered together, they form a kind of national literary totality and present two ways of viewing the national disaster.

Although Sábato rejects the idea of a closely knit generation of contemporary Argentine writers, there are nevertheless a number of other novelists at the present time who are equally concerned with the lot of modern man and with the fate of Argentina. One of the most prolific of these is the novelist, Eduardo Mallea. In his *Historia de una pasión argentina* Mallea divides his country into two parts: the "visible" Argentina

which gives an appearance of vitality as it substitutes a fictitious world for a true one, and the authentic "invisible" Argentina made up of simple working folk who are true to themselves and to the labor which is assigned to them. Hortensia
Paz and the truck driver Bucich of *Sobre héroes y tumbas* could
easily fit Mallea's definition of the "invisible" Argentine from
which the nation ultimately must draw its strength and its
vitality. In most of his novels Mallea depicts the anguished
struggle of solitary souls who are victims of the same overwhelming forces which confront Sábato's protagonists. There
is, in short, a great deal to be said concerning the thematic
parallel to be found in the writings of Mallea and Sábato, but
most of their kinship is certainly due to the fact that they were
born, respectively, in 1903 and 1911 in a nation which was
soon to experience the turmoil of basic political and social upheaval.

Other leading contemporary writers who may be grouped at
least spiritually within the same fold as Sábato include Julio
Cortázar, Marco Denevi, Héctor A. Murena, Norah Lange,
and Julio Ardiles Gray. The fact that each of these figures
chooses some aspect of the common spiritual crisis for special
study in no way makes him less a member of the group. While
Sábato is the first to belie the existence of a formal literary
generation, the fact remains that a great number of the intelligentsia of Argentina today consider him the spokesman of
the new generation. In the words of Ardiles Gray, Sábato's
importance is expressed in this manner: "If anyone of my generation lasts in the literary world, it will be Sábato."[3] It is
Sábato's primary concern for the fate of man that will make
his works endure the test of time. Petersen reaches this conclusion with the following statement: ". . . as long as critics,
or students, or readers remain interested in man as the most
significant reality on the earth, and as long as there is any
kind of public interest in man's lot as he knew it and described
it in the mid-Twentieth Century, then the works of Ernesto
Sábato will exist as significant landmarks in man's artistic and
imaginative description and definition of himself and of his
circumstances."[4]

Any conclusions which Sábato reaches are the result of an
arduous journey through countless pages. The most complete

statements of his thought are to be found in *Sobre héroes y tumbas* and in the volume of essays, *El escritor y sus fantasmas*. His first novel, *El túnel*, is also a broad novelistic statement of the same thesis developed in the essay, *Hombres y engranajes*, but the essentially negative nature of its conclusions makes it atypical of its author's total philosophy. *El túnel* is nevertheless a synthesis of the themes developed more fully in *Sobre héroes y tumbas*. His successive novels are, so to speak, like cities built on the ruins of their predecessors; although new, they enshrine a certain immortality passed on by legends from the past and by the descendants of the original inhabitants. In this way María prefigures Alejandra, and Castel is the prototype of Fernando. Blindness, insanity, incest, and solitude—all major themes in the second novel—are first announced in *El túnel*. The burden of past history on the present is nowhere better expressed than in the history of the Olmos Acevedo family, of which Fernando and Alejandra are the last representatives, and in the epic recounting of the retreat of Juan Lavalle and his legion toward Bolivia. In the first chapter of the present study it is indicated that within all of Sábato's fiction and in certain of the essays the basic idea of a journey is present. This idea first appears in the preface of *Uno y el universo* and is apparent in many other collections of essays. In *El túnel* the journey theme is continued as Castel takes the reader along a one-way street of no return which terminates in his insanity. Since he narrates the entire novel, there is no other point of view from which the reader is able to assess the events described.

All four of the protagonists of *Sobre héroes y tumbas* embark on journeys of self-discovery. Fernando's obsessive quest for an answer to the problems which life dealt him leads him on a symbolic journey not unlike the one taken by Juan Pablo Castel, nor is the end result essentially different. Fernando's physical death closely parallels Castel's complete spiritual and physical isolation as he views an indifferent Buenos Aires from the small window of his jail cell. Alejandra, on the other hand, travels in search of a means of cleansing her body and soul of the accumulated filth of generations. While she primarily represents only herself, she is at the same time the last member of the Olmos Acevedo family, and after her fiery purification

the family becomes extinct except for her aging great-grandfather.

Bruno together with Martín engages in a great deal of soul-
searching, and through his recollections of his association with
the Vidal Olmos family in Capitán Olmos and later in Buenos
Aires much of the mystery surrounding the action is clarified.
At the same time, Bruno is able to understand himself better
and to define his own relationship to Fernando, Ana María,
Georgina, and finally to Alejandra. Although his journey along
the road to self-discovery produces positive results, it remains
for Martín del Castillo to make the most rewarding journey
of the entire novel. It is possible to consider his pilgrimage in
search of himself on two different levels, a spiritual one and a
physical one. On the first level he is no different from the other
protagonists or from Juan Pablo Castel in that he experiences
a series of overwhelming adversities which lead him to the
brink of suicide. Martín, however, is more fortunate; unlike
Castel, Fernando, and Alejandra, he is able to garner a degree
of hope from the tragic events which surround him. Shored
up by the positive approach to life exemplified by Hortensia
Paz and Bucich, he undertakes a journey with the latter to
Patagonia where the glories of existence are revealed to him
in concrete fashion. In Patagonia Martín is to rediscover the
forgotten human qualities within himself, and upon his return
to Buenos Aires he seeks out Bruno for the purpose of making
a detailed analysis of the enigmatic affair he has had with
Alejandra.

There is still another arduous journey described in *Sobre
héroes y tumbas*, that of Juan Lavalle toward Bolivia in 1841.
The details of this trek have already been given, but its fundamental relationship to the journey motif must not be overlooked. Like Martín, Lavalle makes both a physical and a
spiritual pilgrimage. One critic even goes so far as to see in
the putrefying remains of the young general's body a symbol
of Argentina, a nation momentarily defeated yet capable of
continuing the struggle to save and preserve its essence and its
indomitable spirit.[5] Although only Lavalle's bones and heart
make the final leg of the journey, his flesh flows back to its
native soil to be reincarnated into the living flora of the nation.
The goal of Lavalle's journey is thereby realized on a panoram-

ic scale, but on a purely personal basis the sojourn of Martín del Castillo is equally productive. This is nowhere more evident than in the symbolism of Martín's last name; he is the "castle" in which the mustard seed of hope is to be nurtured and preserved.

Intercalated as it is in the fourth part of the novel with Martín's journey to Patagonia, the Lavalle episode gives the novel a degree of polarity which otherwise would be absent. While Sábato's second novel may be considered *the* novel of Buenos Aires, it does acquire in the fourth part a sense of geographical unity and a truly national outlook. While it is Sábato's conviction that it would take many novels to describe the confused reality of Argentina—the decadent oligarchy, the obsolescent gaucho, the struggling immigrant, and the cosmopolitan inhabitant of Buenos Aires—*Sobre héroes y tumbas* comes much closer to this goal in the opinion of the present writer than any other single novel. Sábato's definition of the components of a national novel does a great deal toward clarifying the sources of his own two novels:

> And perhaps the most complex psychological and metaphysical figure of the contemporary Argentine novel is the descendant of foreigners, that strange creature whose blood comes from Genoa or Toledo but whose life has transpired on the Argentine pampas or in the streets of this Babylonian city. What is my country?
> . . . .
> One's country is nothing but his childhood, some faces, some memories of adolescence, a tree or a certain district, an insignificant street, an old tango played on a winter's afternoon, the smell (the memory of the smell) of the old motor in the mill, a children's game. (*Escritor*, p. 38)

Two basic conclusions concerning the Argentine novel are apparent from the preceding statement: the integration of many foreign elements into the national complex is probably the most difficult task which the contemporary Argentine novel faces, and an analysis of the nation is inevitably linked to the childhood memories of the novelist. As the son of Italian immigrants, Sábato is well prepared to discuss the role of this significant segment in national affairs. The vicissitudes of the D'Arcángelo family in the second novel emerge as an episode close to the heart of Sábato's own experiences in Rojas. The D'Arcángelos are but one family in a vast array of foreigners who populate *Sobre héroes y tumbas*, and it is this problem which differentiates the River Plate novel from that of Mexico and the Andean region where the integration of indigenous elements has long been a major novelistic theme. In the case of Sábato his interest in the immigrant problem is directly related to the second observation made above regarding the contemporary Argentine novel. He as a child was not without problems in this respect, and the resentment which many of his peers vented toward the *gringos* was one aspect in the long line of antagonisms described later in *El otro rostro del peronismo*. A great deal more may be said concerning the role of Sábato's childhood in his essays and novels. Autobiographical elements abound in *Sobre héroes y tumbas*, especially in the scenes which take place in Capitán Olmos. The adolescent Bruno confused by the events of 1930 in Buenos Aires is directly related to the adolescent Sábato who was a student in nearby La Plata at the same time.

Sensorial stimuli are prominent in Sábato's analysis of the novel, for it is by this means that many bygone memories are stirred from the depths of oblivion to blossom forth in pages of his fiction. The sounds and smells of Rojas are not unlike the crumbs of the *petite madelaine* and the odor of hawthorne which evoke memories of Proust's childhood in *A la recherche du temps perdu*. Both the work of Proust and Sábato's lengthy second novel grow out of the childhood of their respective authors and represent, as it were, a long journey in search of the inner self of their creators. While the relationship of Proust to his mother is well documented, there is little information available to suggest anything concrete regarding Sábato's relationship to his parents or the possibility of this relationship having influenced his novels. He does speak of the strict family background from which he came and of the nostalgia for his mother when he first went to La Plata, but the projection of these feelings into his protagonists must be done only on the basis of conjecture.

Closely related to Sábato's theory that the novel is a direct outgrowth of the childhood experiences of the novelist is his insistent election of the crises of life—the end of childhood, the end of adolescence, the end of life itself—as the major themes of his writings. To this list of personal crises faced by every man should be added the universal crisis of the twentieth century in which the powerful forces of science and reason were almost to snuff out the dim flicker of spiritual values which man vainly tried to preserve. While the early volumes of essays devote most of their attention to the problem of man in a world dominated by science and reason, the degradation of Argentine man because of certain events in the nation's history after 1930 is the subject of *El otro rostro del peronismo* and *El caso Sábato*. This whole problem on a more universal level is the major theme of *El túnel*, and Juan Pablo Castel is the victim, so to speak, of the gross materialism of his age.

Science and mathematics,—two disciplines which dominated Sábato's thinking during his years as a student, — were closely related to his own spiritual crises first in La Plata, later in Paris, and then in Cambridge, Massachusetts. Momentarily the world of reason was to come to Sábato's rescue when he underwent his "end-of-childhood" crisis upon first arriving in La Plata. Later, as a confused adolescent in Paris, he was to retreat into a world of mathematical precision as a refuge from the conflicting political currents in which he found himself. The fact that Sábato emerged as a novelist from such an anguished scientific beginning is indeed remarkable. No small part of this is due to the interest and encouragement which Sábato received from his professor in La Plata, the Dominican scholar, Pedro Henríquez Ureña, who spent his great literary talents in the correction of the homework of his insignificant secondary school students in the hope that among them there might be a future writer. In 1940 Henríquez Ureña discovered the potential he had been seeking in a former student of his, one Ernesto Sábato, and he offered to take one of his articles to the journal *Sur* and to recommend its publication. The influence of the Dominican professor on the literary career of Sábato should never be discounted; without his introduction of the young writer to the literary world, Sábato's debut as a major writer might have been indefinitely postponed.

In *Sobre héroes y tumbas* all of the major crises of life are evident in one form or another. The experiences of Bruno, himself a sometime writer, more closely parallel Sábato's own personal crises, although in all truth there are moments when Fernando, Alejandra, and Martín seem to undergo crucial events not unlike those Sábato had known in Rojas, in La Plata, and later in Europe. With Bruno the reader is able to follow the thread of life from his childhood in Capitán Olmos, the fictional representation of Rojas, to his days as a student in Buenos Aires and finally through the unsettled years of the 1930's up to the present. Bruno's crises are Sábato's, but at the same time the reader must remember that the end of Martín's adolescence described so vividly in the novel and the dark pages of Fernando's life are also chapters taken from Sábato's own autobiography. Finally, Fernando and Alejandra and even Juan Pablo Castel are to come face to face with the greatest crisis in a positive manner, and while it is unknown exactly how Martín del Castillo will react when death finally arrives at his doorstep, he at least finds a philosophy of life which dissipates the almost total darkness in which Sábato's other characters lived.

There is a good case for comparing the darkness of the world of Fernando and of certain other characters with the obsessive theme of blindness first evident in *El túnel* and developed to the point of psychopathic concern in the second novel. Sábato's affirmation that he himself is the victim of such an obsession establishes a very personal aspect to the whole Fernando episode, but it would most certainly be an error to interpret these facts to mean that Sábato in any way reaches the degree of mental derangement seen in the father of Alejandra. There most certainly are grounds for investigating the possible sources of this obsession in the author's childhood, and Bruno's relation of Fernando's penchant for blinding birds during the days of their youth in Capitán Olmos may indeed provide a key to Sábato's own obsession with blindness. On a broader plane, the "Informe sobre ciegos" is an effort to present the totality of Fernando's personality, and there is no reason to eliminate his greatest obsession from the picture. In the opinion of the present writer there is justification for extending the blindness theme to include the idea of blindness of spiritual values of life on both an individual and a national basis. Martín with the invaluable assistance of Hortensia Paz and Bucich is able to perceive the light of hope through all this darkness and is, so to speak, the best example of one of Sábato's protagonists who is finally able to overcome the world of utter despondency and darkness.

The frequent use of dreams and dream sequences in Sábato's novels is a technique used to formalize the irrational world through which his characters pass. In a sense, they represent windows in the darkness which allow the reader to comprehend actions which would otherwise be meaningless to him. It must be remembered that Sábato passed through the portals of Surrealism, and although he rejected the ultimate consequences of the movement, he did retain a great degree of its interest in the irrational world as it was frequently portrayed through a dream sequence. Only when the Surrealists reached the point of declaring that the true world was the world of the irrational did Sábato reject them just as he had rejected the dogmatic rationalists at an earlier date. For the author of *El túnel* the world must be, in the final analysis, a synthesis of these two extreme points of view. Man is neither pure reason nor pure irrationality; he is somewhere between the extremes of the scientist and the Surrealist on an enigmatic plane of human existence.

As one penetrates the curtain surrounding the world of Sábato, he encounters an abnormal amount of Oedipal involvement in almost all of his major characters. As in the case of *El túnel*, the mother-son attachment often is one in which the would-be feminine lover assumes a mother-figure role in the eyes of her partner. There is no other way to describe the relationship of María to Juan Pablo Castel. In addition, María is a name fraught with religious maternal symbolism, and the reader cannot help but carry the symbol another step by noting that the initials of the Son of the biblical Mary are the same as the first and last initials of Juan Pablo Castel. This theme, so prominently announced in *El túnel*, is the focal point of most of the action of *Sobre héroes y tumbas*, where the central Oedipal situation again involves a feminine character with the name María. It is Ana María, the mother of Fernando, who chronologically begins the Oedipal chain reaction in Sábato's second novel. A great deal of Fernando's intense jealousy, a characteristic which dominates Castel's relationship with María, can be traced directly to the abnormal, possessive love which he felt for his mother. Bruno, orphaned at the age of two years, also looked to Ana María as a maternal symbol during his childhood in Capitán Olmos. Thus, from an early point in their association, Fernando and Bruno are rivals, so to speak, for the affection of the same woman. With the death of Ana María this love is projected by both youths to Georgina, who closely resembles her aunt. Bruno, therefore, is frustrated at every turn by Fernando, who jealously seeks total possession first of his mother and second of the person who physically resembles her.

This Oedipal cycle is carried to a third level in the case of Alejandra, Georgina's daughter whom Fernando has fathered. Bruno's attachment to Alejandra is only momentary, for he quickly realizes that it is merely a projection of his frustrated love for her mother. The relationship between Alejandra and her father, however, is one long Oedipal nightmare with over-tones of a deep-seated Electra complex. It is the veritable key to all the personal relationships in *Sobre héroes y tumbas*. Even Martín's relationship to Alejandra has a maternal aspect. It should be remembered that Martín has always been aware of his mother's desire to abort from the very moment of his accidental conception.

Oedipal involvement completely dominates Alejandra and Fernando, and its influence on Martín and Bruno to a lesser degree can also be observed. Solutions to such complex psychological maladjustments are usually effected only with the aid of prolonged therapy, something apparently unavailable to Sábato's creations, but Alejandra and Fernando do ultimately escape from their twisted affair through death and subsequent symbolic purification. The psychological need for a means to cleanse her body and soul of the accumulated dregs of degeneracy is evident from Alejandra's statements early in the novel, but prolonged baths at various times only remove the exterior soil and leave the spiritual stain untouched.

Alejandra's intense need for spiritual purification is closely related to the same need expressed by Martín and ultimately achieved by him in the cold, virgin plains of Patagonia. Although Fernando never expresses a desire for any type of purification, he is inevitably drawn to the final fatal encounter with Alejandra which is to produce his death and the immolation of both himself and his daughter in the ruins of the Olmos Acevedo house in Barracas. Occuring as it does in May, 1953, it antedates by some two years the fiery baptism of the city of Buenos Aires predicted by El Loco Barragán in Chichín's pizzeria. Purification and physical destruction are one and the same thing for Alejandra, Fernando, and the city in which they live and die, but for Martín del Castillo it is a way of life and salvation.

It is through Hortensia Paz and Bucich that the only positive approach to life and its enigmatic problems is developed. Any hope for relief from the awesome burdens which life in the twentieth century gives man to bear is evident in Sábato's earlier writings only momentarily in the essay, *Hombres y engranajes*. Hope as an ingredient in man's existence is completely absent from *El túnel*, but as Martín is to lift himself from the depths of despair with the aid of a simple girl from the provinces and a truck driver, so was the darkness of Sábato's philoshopy of life to be pierced by a single ray of hope.

Martín, admittedly not the most convincing of Sábato's fictional creations, is nevertheless the vehicle for revealing his creator's most definitive statement to date on what man must do to survive in the machine age. It is Martín's lot to find the key to the Pandora's box which science and reason have created. But in consideration of the profound problems which Martín faces, the solution may seem insignificant and overly simple. Hortensia's answer is to find satisfaction in the simple surroundings in which she finds herself and to dedicate herself to the role which life assigned her to play. Bucich extends this philoshopy to include an appreciation of the physical grandeur of his country and to recognize its immense potential. These "invisible" Argentines, as Eduardo Mallea would call them, are the reserves on which Argentina must ultimately rely if it is to build a truly great nation in the austral corner of the earth on which the drama of its future is yet to be played.

Stylistically, all of Sábato's writings are characterized by a high degree of clarity which, although somewhat obscured by the multiplicity of his approach in the second novel, sets him apart as a true master of the tongue of Cervantes. There is little doubt that his early training in science and mathematics had a great deal to do with the evolution of such a style. *Uno y el universo* and *Heterodoxia* both show evidence of a mind with a scientific orientation in the unnecessarily precise manner in which they are organized. *El túnel* and even *Sobre héroes y tumbas* show moments of almost pure dialecticism as Castel, Fernando, and occasionally Martín analyze the events in which they are ensnared. It is not uncommon to find the various alternatives to a problem numbered and listed as if they were the result of scientific analysis.

While many of the characteristics of Sábato's style are evident in his early essays and in *El túnel*, it was in *Sobre héroes y tumbas* that his technique reached its full maturity. One critic has described the latter novel as a musical composition in four movements with the highest degree of dissonance evident in the "Informe sobre ciegos" and with the melancholy themes of the first movement reappearing and reaching a climax in the fourth.[6] The multiplicity of themes already evident as a result of the present study is duplicated as one considers the many ways by which Sábato presents his view of life to his readers. Here one is reminded of the presentation employed by William Faulkner in which reality is partially revealed by each of the characters as well as by the author himself. Sábato openly admits that many of the ramifications of his novels were not evident to him at the time of their writing but that they later were pointed out to him by critics and the reading public. A great deal of the characters' thoughts is made available to the reader through the use of interior monologues in which the essayistic style of Sábato's early works can still be seen. At times these thoughts evolve as a kind of stream-of-consciousness revelation, but at other times they occur parallel to other conversations taking place. In the case of the latter technique, Sábato often uses italics to differentiate between the dialogue and the thoughts of the third party, and in the first edition there are times when the two kinds of type form parallel but contingent columns on the printed page. Subsequent editions have failed to preserve this sytem of page arrangement, often printing the thoughts of the observer in separate sentences scattered throughout the dialogue. Even some of his dialogues in the second novel become veritable essays, and through the use of a large amount of indirect discourse the thoughts of many other characters are frequently injected into a conversation.

Throughout all of Sábato's fiction there is an air of unreality present, due in no small measure to the ecumenical technique of his writing. Immediately the reader is taken into many separate worlds, Sábato's world and those seen and experienced by his creations. The traditional photographic Realism of the omnipresent nineteenth-century writer has been replaced by a kind of magical Realism in which the inner world of the individual reflects the whole of the universe. In sum, the universe is within each of Sábato's characters and within Sábato himself.

There can be no doubt that the principal value of Sábato's essays and novels is the fact that he focuses his interest on the spiritual problems of modern man lost in an inhospitable world dominated by science and reason. Man is, therefore, the point of departure in all of his writings. Sábato begins on a general level by seeking to identify man's destiny and role in the confusing events of the twentieth century, but he also considers the same problems on a national level by attempting to synthesize the spiritual crisis of Argentina since 1930. Finally, he turns his attention to the individual man and to the crises of life universally faced by all: the end of childhood, the end of adolescence, the end of life itself. *Sobre héroes y tumbas* stands as a literary monument in which Sábato takes all of these themes presented earlier in his essays and in *El túnel* and develops an answer for the first time to the problems he has presented. Man must reject science and reason as the solution to the problems of society and reaffirm an interest in the human dignity of the individual. Mass society must give way to the solitary soul and allow him to become the center of attention. Likewise, on a national level Argentina can no longer disregard the "invisible" peasant or the factory worker if it is to achieve the greatness its past heroes envisioned, and in the final analysis each human being must dedicate himself to the task life has assigned him.

Sábato's major contribution to literature is his creation of novels and essays of a metaphysical dimension unknown in earlier Spanish American letters. His masterpiece, *Sobre héroes y tumbas*, stands as *the* novel of Buenos Aires and without a doubt is the most representative national novel of Argentina written in the twentieth century. Sábato has successfully attempted to integrate the historical, geographical, and demographic elements of contemporary Argentina into a unified novel which better than any other answers the question: What is Argentina? At the same time he and a large number of other contemporary Spanish American literary figures who, realizing that someday they would have to reach the level of the universal if their writings were to receive more than limited attention, have cast aside the restrictive bonds of the regional novel of social protest and the novel in which the physical setting assumed the role of the protagonist. The struggle for national identity in the emergent nations of Spanish America also has inspired countless novels, but the universal implications in this search for a nation were overlooked until recent years. While the satisfaction of man's physical needs will always be of concern to the human race, it is equally necessary to consider the spiritual needs which the exterior world creates. Ernesto Sábato and others of a similar persuasion have done just that, and the problems of universal and national dimension have come to be those of the individual man struggling to comprehend the role in life which fate has dealt him.

Notes and References

Preface

1. Annually the municipality of Buenos Aires recognizes an outstanding literary contribution with a Municipal Prize.

Chapter One

1. The term *gringo* is usually employed in Argentina to designate Italians or those of Italian ancestry.

2. Titles of Sábato's essays and novels are left in the original Spanish although short titles are used for bibliographical references in the text. All translations of quotations are the work of the present writer except for those quoted from the Knopf translation of *El túnel*. For the convenience of readers not familiar with Spanish a translation of the titles considered in this study is herewith provided: *Uno y el universo* (*One and the Universe*); *El túnel*, translated by Harriet de Onís as *The Outsider* (New York: Alfred A. Knopf, Inc., 1950); *Hombres y engranajes* (*Men and Gears*); *Heterodoxia* (*Heterodoxy*); *El otro rostro del peronismo* (*The Other Face of Peronism*); *El caso Sábato* (*Sábato's Case*); *Sobre héroes y tumbas* (*Concerning Heroes and Tombs*); *El escritor y sus fantasmas* (*The Writer and His Ghosts*); and *Tango, Discusión y clave* (*Tango, Discussion and Key*). There is an unpublished novel called "La fuente muda" (*The Mute Fountain*) from which Sábato abstracted fragments for the journal *Sur* and for *Sobre héroes y tumbas*.

3. *El escritor y sus fantasmas*, pp. 10–11.

4. *Sur*, No. 157 (November 1947), pp. 24–65.

5. "On Alfvén's Hypothesis of a 'Cosmic Cyclotron,'" *Physical Review*, Vol. 55, No. 2 (June 15, 1939), 1272–73.

6. Nelly Cortés, "El escritor 'inconforme' Ernesto Sábato," *Indice de Artes y Letras*, XVI, No. 58 (March 1962), 19.

7. María Angélica Correa, "Entrevista a Ernesto Sábato," *Señales*, No. 134 (January 1962), p. 22.

Chapter Two

1. See the dissertation (University of Washington, 1963), "Ernesto Sábato: Essayist and Novelist," p. 32.

2. Petersen, p. 25.

3. Vol. XVI, No. 158 (March 1962), 20.

4. "Ernesto Sábato: *Heterodoxia*," *Sur*, No. 224 (September–October 1953), pp. 129–32.

5. No. 228 (May–June 1954), p. 128.

6. Petersen, p. 86.

7. See the translation by Constance Garnett (New York: Dell Publishing Co., Inc., 1960), p. 28.

8. Vol. XVI, No. 158 (March 1962), p. 20.

9. Octavio A. Hornos Paz, "El escritor frente a sí mismo," *La Nación* (March 29, 1964), p. 4.

Chapter Three

1. See the essay "Soledad y comunicación," in *Heterodoxia*, pp. 49–50.

2. Petersen, p. 117.

3. See "Magical Realism in Spanish American Fiction," *Hispania*, XXXVIII, No. 2 (May 1955), 187–92.

4. Petersen, pp. 145–46.

5. See "Forma y estructura en algunas novelas argentinas contemporáneas,"*Humanitas*, No. 4 (1963), p. 292.

6. For a more detailed study of this topic see Beverly Jean Gibbs's article, "Spatial Treatment in the Contemporary Psychological Novel of Argentina," *Hispania*, XLV, No. 3 (September 1962), 410–14.

Chapter Four

1. See the study of *Sobre héroes y tumbas* by Ángela B. Dellepiane in *Revista Iberoamericana de Bibliografía*, XV, No. 3 (July–September 1965), 226–50.

2. The recording was issued by Phillips and contains excerpts from the Lavalle episode read by Sábato with musical accompaniment by the well-known guitarist, Eduardo Falú.

Chapter Five

1 See Petersen, pp. 195–96.

Chapter Six

1. Based on personal correspondence between Sábato and the present writer.

2. For a more extensive analysis of the role of Aparicio Sosa consult Petersen, p. 205.

Chapter Seven

1. This statement and the others which follow are based on personal correspondence between Sábato and the present writer.

2. Personal correspondence between Sábato and the author.

3. Statement made in a speech given in Tucumán on July 28, 1964.

4. Petersen, p. 225.

5. Héctor Eandi, "Carta a Ernesto Sábato," *Comentario*, X, No. 36 (1963), 74.

6. Dellepiane, p. 233.

Selected Bibliography

PRIMARY SOURCES

Books:

The first edition of each book is given. In cases where quotations in the present study are from other editions, the edition used is given in parenthesis.

Uno y el universo. Buenos Aires: Sudamericana, 1945.

El túnel. Buenos Aires: Sur, 1948.

Hombres y engranajes; Reflecciones sobre el dinero, la razón y el derrumbe de nuestro tiempo. Buenos Aires: Emecé, 1951. (Second edition, October 1951.)

Heterodoxia. Buenos Aires: Emecé, 1953.

El otro rostro del peronismo; Carta abierta a Mario Amadeo. Buenos Aires: López, 1956. (Second edition, August 1956.)

El caso Sábato; Torturas y libertad de prensa; Carta abierta al Gral. Aramburu. Buenos Aires: privately published, 1956.

Sobre héroes y tumbas. Buenos Aires: Fabril, 1961.

Tango: Discusión y clave. Buenos Aires: Losada, 1963.

El escritor y sus fantasmas. Buenos Aires: Aguilar, 1963. (Second edition, 1964.)

Obras de ficción. Buenos Aires: Losada, 1966. (Definitive edition of *El túnel* and *Sobre héroes y tumbas* with an introduction, "Sobre la vida y las ficciones de Ernesto Sábato," by Harley D. Oberhelman.)

Tres aproximaciones a la literatura de nuestro tiempo. Santiago de Chile: Editorial Universitaria, 1968.

Itinerario. Buenos Aires: Sur, 1969.

La convulsión política y social de nuestro tiempo. Buenos Aires: Edicom, 1969.

Articles:

The following bibliography of Sábato's miscellaneous journalistic writings, while not exhaustive, is representative of those articles most characteristic of him as an essayist. A few other articles of interest because of their historical importance in his career are also included.

"Algunas reflexiones sobre el *nouveau roman*," *Sur*, No. 285 (November–December 1963), pp. 42–67.

"Aquella patria de nuestra infancia," *Sur*, No. 237 (November–December 1955), pp. 102–106.

155

"Arte y literature: Realidad y ficción," *El Litoral* (Buenos Aires), January 28, 1962.

"Arthur Stanley Eddington," *Sur*, No. 123 (January 1945), pp. 38–48.

"Borges y Borges el argentino y la metafísica," *Vida Universitaria*, XIV, No. 681 (April 12, 1964), 3–18.

"Contra la parálisis," *Sur*, No. 119 (September 1944), pp. 118–19.

"Cortés Pla: Galileo Galilei," *Sur*, No. 103 (April 1943), pp. 98–101.

"Desagravio a Borges," *Sur*, No. 94 (July 1942), pp. 30–31.

"El caso 'Lolita,'" *Sur*, No. 260 (September–October 1959), p. 57.

"En torno de Borges," *Casa de las Américas*, III, No. 17–18 (1963), pp. 7–12.

"George Gamow: *Mr. Tompkins in Wonderland*," *Sur*, No. 97 (October 1942), pp. 117–19.

"George Russell Harrison: *Atomos en acción*," *Sur*, No. 93 (June 1942), pp. 62–67.

"Julio Rey Pastor, *La ciencia y la técnica en el descubrimiento de América*," *Revista de Filología Hispánica*, IV (1942), pp. 396–99.

"La deidad," *Sur*, No. 268 (January–February 1961), pp. 79–91.

"La fuente muda," *Sur*, No. 157 (November 1947), pp. 24–65.

"La única paz admisible," *Sur*, No. 129 (July 1945), pp. 28–43.

"Los relatos de Jorge Luis Borges," *Sur*, No. 125 (March 1945), pp. 69–75.

"Luca Pacioli: *La Divina Proporción*," *Sur*, No. 142 (August 1946), pp. 90–99.

"Manuel Gálvez: *Vida de Sarmiento*; Renée Pereyra Olazábal: *Mitre*," *Sur*, No. 129 (July 1945), pp. 114–16.

"Max Planck: ¿*Adónde va la ciencia?*" *Sur*, No. 84 (September 1941), pp. 67–70.

"On Alfvén's Hypothesis of a 'Cosmic Cyclotron,'" *Physical Review*, Vol. 55, No. 12 (June 15, 1939), pp. 1272–1273.

"Palabras, palabras, palabras," *Sur*, No. 267 (November–December 1960), pp. 38–41.

"Realidad y realismo en la literatura de nuestro tiempo," *Comentario*, No. 33 (1962), pp. 10–21.

"Significado de Pedro Henríquez Ureña," *La Gaceta* (Tucumán, Argentina), September 5, 1965.

"Sobre el derrumbe de nuestro tiempo," *Sur*, No. 192–194 (October–November–December 1950), pp. 86–92.

"Sobre el sentido común," *Sur*, No. 121 (November 1944), pp. 64–65.

"Sobre *Heterodoxia*," *Sur*, No. 228 (May–June 1954), p. 128.

"Sobre la metafísica del sexo," *Sur*, No. 209–210 (March–April 1952), pp. 24–47; and No. 213–214 (July–August 1952), pp. 158–61.

"Sobre 'Norteamérica la hermosa,'" *Sur*, No. 195–96 (January–February 1951), pp. 67–69.

"Tango, canción de Buenos Aires," *Negro sobre Blanco*, No. 29 (1963), pp. 19–22.

"Ucar, Maya y Otero: *El gran parto*," *Sur*, No. 198 (April 1951), pp. 72–73.

Translations:

The following translations are of *El túnel:*
The Outsider. New York: Knopf, 1950.
Tunneln. Stockholm: Skoglunds Bokförlag, 1951.
Le Tunnel. Paris: Gallimard, 1956.
Der Maler und das Fenster. Vienna: Rohrer, 1958.
O tunel. Rio de Janeiro: Editôra Civilização Brasileira, 1961.
Tunel. Warsaw: PIW, 1963.
Tunel Samoty. Bratislava: Lub, 1965.
TunelLul. Bucharest: Editura P. L. U., 1965.
An Italian edition by Feltrinelli (Milan) is forthcoming, and fragments have appeared in the Japanese newspaper, Akoku Nippo.

Four translations of *Sobre héroes y tumbas* have been published:
Sopra eroi e tombe. Milan: Feltrinelli, 1965
Bohaterach i Grobach. Warsaw: PIW, 1966.
Alejandra. Paris: Editions du Seuil, 1967.
Über Helden und Gräber. Wiesbaden: Limes Verlag, 1967.
An English translation by Holt, Rinehart and Winston is soon to appear.

Recordings:

Retirada y Muerte de Lavalle. Buenos Aires: Philips, 1965.
Sábato reads excerpts from the Lavalle episode of *Sobre héroes y tumbas;* musical accompaniment is by Eduardo Falú, Mercedes Sosa, and the chorus of Francisco Javier Ocampo.
Ernesto Sábato por él mismo. Autobiografía. Buenos Aires: AMB Discográfica, 1967. Fragments of *Sobre héroes y tumbas, Hombres y engranajes, Uno y el universo*, and *El túnel* as read by Sábato.

SECONDARY SOURCES

Writings About Sábato

AZANCOT, LEOPOLDO. "*El escritor y sus fantasmas*," *Indice de Artes y Letras*, XVII, No. 186 (July 1964), 31. A review of Sábato's ideas concerning literature, the role of art, and the writings of Jorge Luis Borges.

BRUNO, RICARDO. "Ernesto Sábato habla fuerte y claro," *Leoplán* (1964). An interview in which Sábato discusses his novels, current literature, and some of his future plans.

BRUSHWOOD, J. S. "Ernesto Sábato: *Hombres y engranajes,*" *Books Abroad,* Vol. 26, No. 3 (Summer 1952), 281–82. An analysis of one of Sábato's most important essays in which the reviewer relates Sábato's interpretation of life to that of Nicholas Berdyaev and Jean Paul Sartre.

BUONOCORE, DOMINGO. "*El escritor y sus fantasmas,* por Ernesto Sábato," *Universidad,* No. 58 (1964), 416–17. Summarizes Sábato's latest collection of essays with a general evaluation of him as an essayist more than as a novelist.

CANAL FEIJÓO, BERNARDO. "En torno a una 'nouvelle' de Ernesto Sábato," *Escritura,* III, No. 7 (1949), 98–101. Analyzes *El túnel* with special consideration of the enigmatic personality of Juan Pablo Castel.

———. "Ernesto Sábato: *Sobre héroes y tumbas,*" *Sur,* No. 276 (May–June 1962), 90–99. An extensive analysis and interpretation of the second novel and especially valuable for its consideration of the role of abnormal psychology in the work.

CASTILLO, ABELARDO. "*Sobre héroes y tumbas,*" *Índice de Artes y Letras,* XVI, No. 167 (December 1962), 31–32. Important analytical review of Sábato's second novel in which the author compares it with other works of contemporary literature.

CORDERO, NESTOR LUIS. "A la búsqueda de la realidad," *Entrega* (May 1962), 8. A review of *Sobre héroes y tumbas* in which the critic finds a fundamental weakness in the delineation of the novel's heroes.

CORTÉS, NELLY. "El escritor 'inconforme' Ernesto Sábato," *Índice* de *Artes y Letras,* XVI, No. 158 (March 1962), 19–20. Biography and general survey of Sábato's writings followed by an interview in which he answers questions concerning his essays and novels.

DELLEPIANE, ÁNGELA B. "Del barroco y las modernas técnicas en Ernesto Sábato," *Revista Iberoamericana de Bibliografía,* XV, No. 3 (July–September 1965), 226–50. An analysis of *Sobre héroes y tumbas* from the point of view of the multiplicity of its themes and a comparison of it with *El túnel.*

———. *Ernesto Sábato, El hombre y su obra.* New York: Las Américas Publishing Company, 1969. One of the most complete studies of Sábato and his literary works. Contains a valuable bibliography.

"Diálogo con Ernesto Sábato," *El Escarabajo de Oro,* No. 5 (February 1962), 4–6, 20. Sábato discusses his writings and gives his thoughts on contemporary literature in general.

EANDI, HÉCTOR. "Carta a Ernesto Sábato," *Comentario,* X, No. 36 (1963), 71–74, 79. In a letter ostensibly directed to Sábato the author analyzes the themes and the four major protagonists of *Sobre héroes y tumbas.*

"Ensayo sobre la canción proteña," *La Nación* (Buenos Aires), August 8, 1964. A summary of Sábato's essay which includes many of the disparate ideas on the "song of Buenos Aires" found within the volume.

FERNÁNDEZ SUÁREZ, ÁLVARO. "Ernesto Sábato: *Heterodoxia,*" *Sur*, No. 224 (September–October 1953), 129–32. A rather unfavorable review of Sábato's second volume of essays which at the same time praises his ability to present and sustain philosophic ideas.

———. "Ernesto Sábato: *Hombres y Engranajes,*" *Sur*, No. 204 (October 1951), pp. 71–74. Analyzes the essay in terms of its concern for man and his feelings of desperation and isolation in a rational world; the critic concludes with the opinion that Sábato's solution to the problem presented is obscure.

FLORES, ÁNGEL. "Magical Realism in Spanish American Fiction," *Hispania*, XXXVIII, No. 2 (May 1955), 187–92. Discusses the technique of magical Realism in Western literature and treats *El túnel* as a representative work of this movement.

GIBBS, BEVERLY J. "'El túnel': Portrayal of Isolation," *Hispania*, XLVIII, No. 3 (September 1965), 429–36. An analytical study of *El túnel* as a portrayal of Juan Pablo Castel's existential isolation.

———. "Spatial treatment in the Contemporary Psychological Novel of Argentina," *Hispania*, XLV, No. 3 (September 1962), 410–14. A discussion of the novels of Bianco, Mallea, Sábato, Canto, and Mazzanti which develops the theory that spaciality forms a background against which the personalities of the protagonists are delineated; Castel and *El túnel* are analyzed from this point of view.

GONZÁLEZ, ABELARDO. "*El túnel,*" *Sur*, No. 211–12 (May–June 1952), 163–65. Evaluates the film version of *El túnel* in which Sábato colaborated with the director, León Klimovsky, to produce a motion picture of outstanding merit, especially in regard to its interpretation of the role of Buenos Aires in the original story.

GUDIÑO KRAMER, L. "*Sobre héroes y tumbas*, por Ernesto Sábato," *Universidad*, No. 58 (1963), 406–408. A good analysis of the second novel from the standpoint of the four plot divisions and of the symbolism of the several protagonists.

HARRIS, YVONNE J. "Ernesto Sábato: *El túnel,*" *Books Abroad*, Vol. 26, No. 2 (Spring 1952), 185. An excellent short review of *El túnel*, which points out the novel's emphasis on the tortured and incoherent workings of Castel's neurotic mind.

HAYES, ALFRED. "A Misunderstood Criminal," New York *Herald Tribune*, May 14, 1950. A general analysis of Sábato's first novel based on the English translation published in 1950.

Hornos Paz, Octavio A. El escritor frente a sí mismo," *La Nación*, March 29, 1964, 4. A critical analysis of the three textual divisions of *El escritor y sus fantasmas*.

Jones, Willis K. "Ernesto Sábato: *Uno y el universo*," *Books Abroad*, Vol. 20, No. 3 (Summer 1946), 321. General analysis of the first volume of essays in which the reviewer concludes that the eighty essays all contain a great deal of common sense.

"Lavalle: una leyenda de Sábato en guitarra criolla," *Confirmado*, May 7, 1965, 45. Sábato's recording is reviewed with a historical and critical analysis of the role of Juan Lavalle in *Sobre héroes y tumbas*.

"Llega Ernesto Sábato," *Índice de Artes y Letras*, XVI, No. 167 (December 1962), 32. Describes Sábato's arrival at Barajas Airport in Madrid and evaluates the writer's personality.

Liberman, Arnoldo. "Carta de Buenos Aires," *Revista de la Universidad de México*, Vol. XVI, No. 5 (January 1962), 20–21. Views Sábato as an active protagonist in the tumultuous events of the twentieth century instead of a detached intellectual.

Lichtblau, Myron. "Forma y estructura en algunas novelas argentinas contemporáneas," *Humanitas*, No. 4 (1963), 285–98. As a part of his study of various contemporary Argentine novels the author makes an analysis of *El túnel* pointing out its picaresque and *tremendista* tendencies.

Lipp, Solomon. "Ernesto Sábato: Síntoma de una época," *Journal of Inter-American Studies*, Vol. VIII, No. 1 (January 1966), 142–55. Probably the best overview of Sábato's essays and novels. Considers all of his writings except for the volumes of essays published after *Sobre héroes y tumbas*.

Olguín, Manuel. "Ernesto Sábato: *Uno y el universo*," *Books Abroad*, Vol. 21, No. 2 (Spring 1947), 201–202. A review of the first volume of essays which the reviewer finds unusual because of its use of science as a springboard to philosophy.

Ortega Peña, Rodolfo. "Letras argentinas," *Ficción*, No. 83 (July–August 1962), 55–57. An analysis of Sábato as a novelist with special consideration of the use of vagueness and suggestivity in the second novel.

Petersen, John Fred. "Ernesto Sábato: Essayist and Novelist," dissertation, University of Washington, 1963. Available from University Microfilms, Inc., Ann Arbor, Michigan. One of the most comprehensive and complete studies of Sábato's works up to the year 1961.

———. "Sábato's 'El Túnel': More Freud than Sartre," *Hispania*, L, No. 2 (May 1967), 271–76. Attempts to relate the content of *El túnel* to a universally valid fact of human psychology: the Oedipus complex.

ROGGIANO, ALFREDO A. "Ernesto Sábato" in *Diccionario de la literatura latinoamericana*. Washington: Pan American Union, 1961. An excellent biography of Sábato and a consideration of his writings up to the second novel. Contains a bibliography of other critical studies.

SÁNCHEZ RIVA, ARTURO. "Ernesto Sábato: *El túnel*," *Sur*, No. 169 (November 1948), 82–87. Castel's personality as the central idea of *El túnel* is the subject of this critical analysis.

———. "Ernesto Sábato: Uno y el universo," *Sur*, No. 135 (January 1946), 101–106. In this analysis of Sábato's first collection of essays the critic views the work as an attempt by man to find truth and his place in life.

Index